Taste of Home
FROSTY
Treats & More

201 COOL IDEAS FOR ICY SWEETS

TASTE OF HOME BOOKS • RDA ENTHUSIAST BRANDS, LLC • MILWAUKEE, WI

Taste of Home
Reader's digest

EDITORIAL
Editor-in-Chief: Catherine Cassidy
Creative Director: Howard Greenberg
Editorial Operations Director: Kerri Balliet

Managing Editor, Print & Digital Books:
Mark Hagen
Associate Creative Director: Edwin Robles Jr.

Editors: Christine Rukavena, Michelle Rozumalski
Art Director: Jessie Sharon
Layout Designer: Catherine Fletcher
Editorial Production Manager: Dena Ahlers
Copy Chief: Deb Warlaumont Mulvey
Copy Editors: Joanne Weintraub, Mary-Liz Shaw
Content Operations Manager: Colleen King
Content Operations Assistant: Shannon Stroud
Executive Assistant: Marie Brannon

Chief Food Editor: Karen Berner
Food Editors: James Schend; Peggy Woodward, RD
Recipe Editors: Mary King; Jenni Sharp, RD; Irene Yeh

Test Kitchen & Food Styling Manager:
Sarah Thompson
Test Cooks: Nicholas Iverson (lead), Matthew Hass,
Lauren Knoelke
Food Stylists: Kathryn Conrad (senior), Leah Rekau,
Shannon Roum
Prep Cooks: Megumi Garcia, Melissa Hansen,
Bethany Van Jacobson, Sara Wirtz

Photography Director: Stephanie Marchese
Photographers: Dan Roberts, Jim Wieland
Photographer/Set Stylist: Grace Natoli Sheldon
Set Stylists: Stacey Genaw, Melissa Haberman,
Dee Dee Jacq

Editorial Business Manager: Kristy Martin
Editorial Business Associate: Samantha Lea Stoeger

BUSINESS
General Manager, Taste of Home Cooking School:
Erin Puariea

THE READER'S DIGEST ASSOCIATION, INC.
President and Chief Executive Officer:
Bonnie Kintzer
Chief Financial Officer: Colette Chestnut
**Vice President, Chief Operating Officer,
North America:** Howard Halligan
Vice President, Enthusiast Brands, Books & Retail:
Harold Clarke
Chief Marketing Officer: Leslie Dukker Doty
Vice President, North American Human Resources:
Phyllis E. Gebhardt, SPHR
Vice President, Brand Marketing: Beth Gorry
Vice President, Global Communications: Susan Russ
Vice President, Chief Technology Officer:
Aneel Tejwaney
Vice President, Consumer Marketing Planning:
Jim Woods

For other Taste of Home books and products,
visit tasteofhome.com.

For more Reader's Digest products and information,
visit rd.com (in the United States) or rd.ca (in Canada).

International Standard Book Number:
978-1-61765-402-2
Library of Congress Control Number:
2014957257

Cover Photographer: Grace Natoli Sheldon
Set Stylist: Stephanie Marchese
Food Stylist: Sarah Thompson

Pictured on front cover: Frozen Sandwich Cookies,
page 147.
Pictured on back cover: Lemon 'n' Lime Strawberry
Ice, page 80, and Ice Cream Cookie Dessert, page 120.
Illustrations on inside cover:
Ohn Mar/Shutterstock.com

Printed in China.
5 7 9 10 8 6 4

 **LIKE US**
facebook.com/tasteofhome

 TWEET US
@tasteofhome

 **FOLLOW US**
pinterest.com/taste_of_home

SHOP WITH US
shoptasteofhome.com

SHARE A RECIPE
tasteofhome.com/submit

Frozen Banana Split Pie, page 116

Coconut Pineapple Pops, page 170

TABLE OF CONTENTS

**Oatmeal Cookie
Ice Cream Sandwiches,**
page 151

**Frozen Fruit
Yogurt Pops,**
page 163

HERE'S THE SCOOP

"I scream…you scream…we all scream…for ice cream!"
Who doesn't love a cool and creamy scoop? Ever-popular ice cream and other frozen favorites are guaranteed hits with people of all ages—and not only when the sun's at its hottest during the height of summer.

Now you and your family can indulge anytime with the delectable desserts, snacks and beverages featured inside *Taste of Home Frosty Treats & More*. Whether served in a cone, stacked in a sandwich, piled into a pie crust or poured into a tall glass, these sweet sensations can't be beat. Flip through this cool collection and whip up a special surprise today!

Try this
**Georgia Peach
Ice Cream**
(page 39).

**Lemon Meringue
Ice Cream Pie,**
page 99

What's
In a Name?

With all the frozen treats sold in the store, you may wonder how they differ. **Here's a rundown of the most popular choices.**

Sip these **Creamy Lemon Milk Shakes** (page 11).

ICE CREAM is Americans' favorite frozen dessert. It typically contains 10 percent butterfat, but premium brands have 11 to 16 percent butterfat for a richer, creamier product.

REDUCED-FAT ICE CREAM used to be called ice milk and contains 25 percent less fat than a brand's regular ice cream.

FROZEN CUSTARD is sometimes called French-style ice cream. It contains 10 percent butterfat and either eggs or egg yolks.

FROZEN YOGURT gets a tart flavor from the yogurt cultures added to the milk mixture. The fat content varies among brands, so read the label if you are looking for a low-fat treat.

GELATO is an Italian-style ice cream. During processing, less air is whipped into it. The result is smoother and denser than American-style ice cream.

SHERBET is made from fruit juice, a milk product, sugar and water. It can also contain fruit, spices or chocolate. It has a lighter texture than ice cream and can be sweeter.

SORBET is made from pureed fruit, fruit juice, sugar and water. It may also contain liqueur or wine. It does not contain milk or eggs.

GRANITAS (Italian), *ganites* (French) and ices are made with water, sugar and fruit juice, wine or coffee. Frequent stirring gives them a grainy texture.

Blueberry Ice Cream, page 67

Let's Get Started!

If you're using an ice cream maker, make sure to read the manufacturer's directions. **Then keep the following tips in mind for sweet success.**

MOST ICE CREAM MIXTURES must be refrigerated before freezing and need to sit in the freezer for about 4 hours before serving. If you refrigerate the mixture overnight rather than for just a few hours, your ice cream will freeze faster and have a smoother texture.

FILL THE CYLINDER of the ice cream freezer no more than two-thirds full. As the paddle stirs the ice cream, air is incorporated and the mixture expands. If the cylinder is too full, the mixture will spill out. When you are transferring the ice cream to the freezer container, do not fill it to the rim—ice cream expands during freezing and may push off the lid.

RECIPES WITH EGGS or egg yolks may call for the ice cream mixture to reach a

consistency that will coat a metal spoon. When a metal spoon is dipped into the hot mixture, it should cling to the spoon. If it doesn't, continue to cook the mixture over low heat.

WHEN MAKING a sorbet, use your food processor to make short work of pureeing the fruit. Also, don't skimp on the amount of sugar listed in the recipe. The high sugar content in sorbets keeps them from freezing into hard cubes of ice. Sugar also helps produce a sorbet's wonderfully smooth texture. So keep things sweet and enjoy!

Serving Secrets

- When scooping ice cream from the carton, do so quickly and return the unused portion to the freezer as soon as possible. Thawing and refreezing ice cream causes ice crystals to form on the surface.

- Having a party? Before guests arrive, scoop ice cream into cupcake liners, place them on a baking sheet and return them to the freezer until serving. You won't have to scoop while guests wait—just remove the liners and place each scoop in a bowl.

- Dress up ice cream cones or waffle cone bowls by dipping the rim into melted chocolate, then rolling it in sprinkles or finely chopped nuts. Let the chocolate set and store in an airtight container.

- Out of ice cream topping? Warm a little jam or jelly in the microwave and drizzle it over scoops. For an adult topping, add coffee-flavored or fruit-flavored liqueur.

- Citrus fruits like oranges, limes and lemons can make festive bowls. Cut the fruit in half and hollow out the rind, reserving the fruit for another use. Fill the shells with ice cream.

For a crispy counterpoint to **Chunky Banana Cream Freeze** on page 61, garnish each scoop with a sugar cookie.

Serve these **Cool Watermelon Pops** (page 159) in an iced watermelon for extra fun.

COOL
BEVERAGES

LEMON MERINGUE PIE COCKTAIL

START TO FINISH: 5 MIN.
MAKES: 1 SERVING

    1   **lemon wedge**
        Coarse yellow and white sugar
1½ to 2 **cups ice cubes**
    3   **ounces limoncello**
    1   **ounce half-and-half cream**
    1   **tablespoon lemon sorbet**
    2   **teaspoons lemon juice**

1. Rub lemon wedge around the rim of a martini glass; dip rim in coarse sugar. Set aside.

2. Fill a shaker three-fourths full with ice. Add the limoncello, cream, sorbet and lemon juice to shaker; cover and shake for 10-15 seconds or until condensation forms on outside of shaker. Strain into prepared glass.

NOTE *To make a Lemon Meringue Pie Mocktail, substitute ⅓ cup lemonade for the limoncello.*

> Don't let the light lemon flavor and rich, creamy texture fool you: This cool, smooth drink is an adults-only indulgence. Limoncello is an Italian lemon liqueur.
> —*TASTE OF HOME* TEST KITCHEN

PEACHY BERRY SHAKES

I love to whip up milk shakes, malts and smoothies on summer afternoons. This fruity shake is refreshingly cool on sweltering days.

—**ADRIENNE HOLLISTER** SULTAN, WA

START TO FINISH: 10 MIN.
MAKES: 4 SERVINGS

    ½   **cup milk**
    3   **cups vanilla ice cream**
1½ **cups fresh or frozen sliced peeled peaches**
    1   **cup fresh or frozen strawberries**
    ¾   **cup vanilla, peach or strawberry yogurt**
        Whipped cream, slivered almonds and whole fresh strawberries

In a blender, combine the milk, ice cream, peaches, strawberries and yogurt; cover and process until smooth. Pour into chilled glasses. Garnish with whipped cream, almonds and strawberries. Serve immediately.

CRANBERRY RASPBERRY PUNCH

Not too sweet, this pretty pink punch offers pure refreshment. My family never tires of it at special occasions throughout the year.

—SUSAN ROGERS WILMINGTON, MA

START TO FINISH: 10 MIN.
MAKES: ABOUT 5 QUARTS

- 2 **packages (10 ounces each) frozen sweetened sliced strawberries**
- 1 **can (12 ounces) frozen lemonade concentrate, thawed**
- 1 **can (11½ ounces) frozen cranberry raspberry juice concentrate, thawed**
- 2 **liters ginger ale, chilled**
- 2 **liters club soda, chilled**
- 1 **quart raspberry or orange sherbet**

In a blender, combine the strawberries, lemonade concentrate and cranberry raspberry concentrate; cover and process until smooth. Transfer to a punch bowl. Gently stir in ginger ale and club soda. Top with scoops of sherbet. Serve immediately.

SERVING SUCCESS

Keep your sherbet scoops small so they're easy to ladle into punch cups or glasses. This recipe serves 20 to 25 guests, depending on the size of your glasses.

CREAMY LEMON MILK SHAKES

Several different recipes inspired the combination of ingredients I use in these shakes, and I'm so glad they did! They're really refreshing.

—CAROL GILLESPIE CHAMBERSBURG, PA

START TO FINISH: 10 MIN.
MAKES: 4 SERVINGS

- 2 tablespoons crushed lemon drop candies
- 1 teaspoon sugar
- ½ small lemon, cut into six slices, divided
- ½ cup 2% milk
- 2 cups vanilla ice cream
- 2 cups lemon sorbet
- 3 ounces cream cheese, softened
- 2 teaspoons grated lemon peel
- ½ teaspoon vanilla extract

1. In a shallow dish, mix crushed lemon drops and sugar. Using 1 or 2 lemon slices, moisten rims of four glasses; dip rims into candy mixture.

2. Place remaining ingredients in a blender; cover and process until smooth. Pour into prepared glasses; serve immediately with remaining lemon slices.

Jungle Float

JUNGLE FLOAT

START TO FINISH: 5 MIN. • **MAKES:** 1 SERVING

- 3 **tablespoons chocolate syrup**
- 3 **scoops chocolate or vanilla ice cream**
- 1 **cup chilled club soda**
  Optional toppings: sliced banana, honey-roasted peanuts, cut-up peanut butter cups, animal crackers, whipped cream and maraschino cherries

Place 2 tablespoons chocolate syrup in a tall glass. Add ice cream and remaining chocolate syrup. Top with club soda. Garnish with toppings of your choice. Serve immediately.

> This fun float lets kids (and the adults, too) be the masters of their own creations. What a tasty way to experiment!
> —**JENNI SHARP** MEQUON, WI

CARAMEL MACCHIATO FLOATS

My absolute favorite coffee drink is a caramel Frappuccino. Because they are pretty costly to buy regularly, I decided to come up with my own version at home. I recently made this for a party; my guests couldn't get enough.

—MELISSA HELLER SANTA MARIA, CA

START TO FINISH: 20 MIN.
MAKES: 8 SERVINGS

- 6 **cups cold brewed coffee**
- 1 **cup 2% milk**
- ⅓ **cup caramel flavoring syrup**
- ¼ **cup sugar**
- 8 **scoops coffee ice cream**
- 8 **scoops dulce de leche ice cream**
  Whipped cream and caramel sundae syrup

In a large pitcher, combine the first four ingredients. Divide ice cream among eight chilled glasses; pour coffee mixture over top. Garnish servings with whipped cream and sundae syrup. **NOTE** *This recipe was tested with Torani brand flavoring syrup. Look for it in the coffee section.*

STRAWBERRY PATCH FROST

Fresh strawberries get a delicious chilled treatment in this pretty drink.

—TASTE OF HOME TEST KITCHEN

START TO FINISH: 5 MIN.
MAKES: 1 SERVING

- 2 **tablespoons strawberry jam**
- 1 **teaspoon water**
- 3 **scoops strawberry ice cream**
- ½ **cup sliced fresh strawberries**
- ¼ **cup heavy whipping cream or half-and-half cream**
- 1 **cup chilled strawberry or raspberry sparkling water**
  Whipped cream
  Colored sprinkles

In a tall glass, combine strawberry jam and water. Add ice cream, strawberries and cream. Top with sparkling water. Garnish with whipped cream and sprinkles. Serve immediately.

MEASURING COFFEE

Most coffeemakers brew a 6-ounce "cup," while the recipes in this chapter call for coffee measured in a traditional 8-ounce cup. To get 6 cups of coffee for the caramel floats recipe, you may need to set your pot to brew 8 cups.

MANGO-GREEN TEA SMOOTHIES

This tropical treat has a refreshing flavor combination that's perfect for hot weather, but it's a yummy pick-me-up anytime.

—*TASTE OF HOME* **TEST KITCHEN**

START TO FINISH: 10 MIN.
MAKES: 2 SERVINGS

1½ **cups frozen chopped peeled mangoes**
½ **cup brewed green tea, chilled**

3 **to 4 tablespoons lime juice**
1 **tablespoon honey**
1 **cup low-fat vanilla frozen yogurt**

In a blender, combine the mangoes, tea, lime juice and honey; cover and process until blended. Add frozen yogurt; cover and process until smooth. Pour into chilled glasses; serve immediately.

CREME DE CACAO

The cacao bean liqueur comes in two types: dark (which is dark brown) and white (which is clear). Choose clear for most recipes so you can control the color.

Grasshopper
Shakes

GRASSHOPPER SHAKES

START TO FINISH: 10 MIN.
MAKES: 10 SERVINGS (2½ QUARTS)

- 2 **quarts vanilla ice cream**
- 1 **carton (8 ounces) frozen whipped topping, thawed**
- ¾ **cup green creme de menthe**
- ¾ **cup creme de cacao**

In a blender, cover and process the ingredients in batches until blended. Stir if necessary. Pour into chilled glasses; serve immediately.

Minty, chocolaty and cool, this spiked dessert drink is a wonderful way to toast family and friends at holiday gatherings. A little shaved chocolate on top adds an extra-festive touch.
—**MARCIA WHITNEY** GAINESVILLE, FL

FROSTY NOTES

_____
_____
_____
_____
_____
_____
_____
_____
_____
_____
_____
_____
_____
_____
_____
_____
_____
_____
_____
_____
_____
_____
_____
_____
_____
_____
_____
_____
_____
_____
_____
_____
_____
_____
_____
_____
_____
_____
_____
_____

RASPBERRY CHEESECAKE FLOATS

START TO FINISH: 15 MIN. • **MAKES:** 6 SERVINGS

- 2 **cans (12 ounces each) cream soda, divided**
- ¼ **teaspoon almond extract**
- 3 **ounces cream cheese, softened**
- 1 **package (12 ounces) frozen unsweetened raspberries**
- 4 **cups vanilla ice cream, softened if necessary, divided**

TOPPINGS

Whipped cream
Fresh blackberries and blueberries

1. Place ½ cup cream soda, extract, cream cheese, raspberries and 2 cups ice cream in a blender; cover and process until smooth.
2. Divide among six tall glasses. Top with remaining ice cream and cream soda. Garnish floats with whipped cream and berries. Serve immediately.

I've yet to meet a cheesecake I didn't like! The flavors of cream cheese and raspberries here are an ideal combination. Although ice cream floats are summery, I like this treat so much that I whip it up during the winter, too.
—**DEIRDRE COX** KANSAS CITY, MO

Raspberry
Cheesecake Floats

PINEAPPLE COLADA SHAKE

With refreshing coconut and pineapple flavors, this frothy shake is sinfully delicious! With its cool, creamy texture, it just begs to be your poolside companion.

—**MELISSA JELINEK** APPLE VALLEY, MN

START TO FINISH: 5 MIN.
MAKES: 1 SERVING

- **¼ cup coconut-flavored rum**
- **½ cup vanilla ice cream**
- **½ cup canned crushed pineapple**

Ground cinnamon
Pineapple wedge and maraschino cherry

Place the rum, ice cream and pineapple in a blender. Cover and process for 30 seconds or until blended. Transfer to a chilled glass. Sprinkle with cinnamon. Garnish with pineapple and cherry.

SPRINGTIME STRAWBERRY MALTS

Don't limit yourself to having a malt only when you go out. This refreshing beverage makes mealtime fun for the whole family.

—TASTE OF HOME TEST KITCHEN

START TO FINISH: 10 MIN.
MAKES: 4 SERVINGS

- ¼ **cup milk**
- 2 **tablespoons strawberry syrup**
- ½ **cup malted milk powder**
- 6 **fresh or frozen strawberries**
- 4 **cups vanilla ice cream, softened**

Place all ingredients in a blender; cover and process until smooth. Pour into chilled glasses. Serve immediately.

ORANGE CREME SODAS

This treat is a hit with kids and adults alike. Serve it on National Creamsicle Day—Aug. 14—or whenever the temperature calls for frosty flavor.

—LILLIAN WEIR DARTMOUTH, NS

START TO FINISH: 10 MIN.
MAKES: 4 SERVINGS

- 8 **scoops vanilla ice cream (¼ cup each)**
- 4 **cups orange soda, chilled**
- ¼ **teaspoon orange extract**

Place two scoops ice cream in each of four chilled 16-oz. glasses. In a pitcher, combine the soda and extract. Pour over ice cream. Serve immediately.

LEMON-PINEAPPLE PUNCH

With pineapple juice and sherbet, this
fresh-tasting punch is perfect for kids
and adults alike on scorching days.

—TASTE OF HOME TEST KITCHEN

START TO FINISH: 20 MIN.
MAKES: 5 QUARTS

- **1 can (46 ounces) unsweetened
  pineapple juice**
- **2 cans (12 ounces each) frozen
  lemonade concentrate, thawed**
- **¼ cup sugar**
- **¼ cup lemon juice**
- **2 liters lemon-lime soda, chilled**
- **2 pints pineapple sherbet, softened**
- **5 drops yellow food coloring,
  optional**
  **Pineapple chunks and maraschino
  cherries, optional**

1. In a punch bowl, combine the
pineapple juice, lemonade concentrate,
sugar and lemon juice. Add the soda,
sherbet and food coloring if desired;
stir until blended.
2. Serve immediately, garnishing
servings with pineapple and cherries
if desired.

ANGEL FROST

I've served this refreshing beverage for
breakfasts and brunches for 20 years.
—SUSAN O'BRIEN SCOTTSBLUFF, NE

START TO FINISH: 5 MIN.
MAKES: 4-6 SERVINGS (ABOUT 1 QUART)

- **¾ cup thawed pink lemonade
  concentrate**
- **1 cup milk**
- **1 package (10 ounces) frozen
  sweetened sliced strawberries,
  partially thawed**
- **1 pint vanilla ice cream**
  Fresh strawberries, optional

Place the first four ingredients in
a blender; cover and process until
smooth. Pour into chilled glasses.
Garnish with strawberries if desired.

IRISH WHISKEY FLOAT

Here's a tasty adult spin on a favorite
childhood ice cream treat. Every sip is
cool, creamy and fun!
—NICK IVERSON BAY VIEW, WI

START TO FINISH: 5 MIN.
MAKES: 1 SERVING

- **1 scoop vanilla ice cream**
- **1 cup cola**
- **1 ounce Irish whiskey**

Place ice cream in a tall glass; top with
cola and whiskey. Serve immediately.

Angel Frost

RASPBERRY POMEGRANATE SMOOTHIES

Avail yourself of raspberry and pomegranate's nutritional benefits by sampling this smoothie. You'll love the unique blend of flavors.

—TASTE OF HOME TEST KITCHEN

START TO FINISH: 10 MIN.
MAKES: 4 SERVINGS

1½ cups pomegranate juice
2 cups frozen unsweetened raspberries
¼ cup packed brown sugar
2 cups low-fat vanilla frozen yogurt

In a blender, combine juice, raspberries and brown sugar; cover and process until blended. Add frozen yogurt; cover and process until blended. Pour into chilled glasses; serve immediately.

CHILLY COFFEE PUNCH

For a twist on the usual fruit punch, try a flavored coffee with ice cream, brought together just before serving.

—JUDY WILSON SUN CITY WEST, AZ

PREP: 10 MIN. + CHILLING
MAKES: 24 SERVINGS

- 6 **cups hot strong brewed coffee**
- ¼ **cup sugar**
- ½ **cup coffee liqueur**
- 1 **carton (1½ quarts) vanilla ice cream, softened**
- 1 **carton (1½ quarts) chocolate ice cream, softened**

Optional toppings: whipped cream, chocolate syrup and chocolate shavings

1. In a pitcher, combine coffee and sugar, stirring to dissolve sugar. Refrigerate, covered, until cold, about 45 minutes.

2. Stir liqueur into coffee. Just before serving, spoon ice cream into a punch bowl. Stir in coffee mixture. If desired, serve with toppings.

FROSTY NOTES

_____

_____

_____

_____

_____

_____

_____

_____

_____

_____

_____

_____

_____

_____

_____

_____

_____

_____

_____

_____

_____

_____

_____

_____

_____

_____

_____

_____

_____

_____

_____

_____

_____

_____

CHERRY MALTS

White chocolate and cherry are a luscious combination in this delightfully frosty malt. For a thicker, fruitier malt, add some frozen sweet cherries to the blender before processing.

—LEAH REKAU EAGLE RIVER, WI

START TO FINISH: 5 MIN. • **MAKES:** 2 SERVINGS

- 1 **cup milk**
- 3 **cups cherry ice cream**
- 3 **tablespoons malted milk powder**
- 1 **ounce white baking chocolate, chopped**

In a blender, combine the milk, ice cream, malted milk powder and chocolate; cover and process until blended. Pour into chilled glasses.

LEMON MINT COOLER

Here's a fizzy refresher that blends lemon sherbet, cool mint and ginger ale. It's sure to hit the spot on a hot afternoon.

—CHAVELYIN MARIE KARLOVICH MONROE, CT

START TO FINISH: 15 MIN.
MAKES: ABOUT 5 CUPS

- 2¼ **cups water**
- ½ **cup coarsely chopped fresh mint**
- ½ **cup lemon juice**
- 2 **medium lemons, sliced**
- ½ **cup lemon sherbet, softened**
- 1 **liter ginger ale, chilled**

For mint ice cubes, combine the water, mint and lemon juice; pour into two ice cube trays. Freeze until set. In a pitcher, combine the lemons and sherbet; slowly stir in ginger ale. Add the mint ice cubes.

Cherry Malts

WHITE CHOCOLATE

White chocolate contains no cocoa solids, so it technically is not chocolate. It does contain cocoa butter, which gives it a rich, buttery texture. Higher-quality white chocolate has a greater percentage of cocoa butter, while imitation chocolate has none.

STRAWBERRY SHAKES

Cool off with a thick, rich treat that will remind you of a malt shop!

—KATHRYN CONRAD TALLAHASSEE, FL

START TO FINISH: 5 MIN.
MAKES: 2 SERVINGS

- ⅓ **cup 2% milk**
- 1½ **cups vanilla ice cream**
- ½ **cup frozen unsweetened strawberries**
- 1 **tablespoon strawberry preserves**

In a blender, combine all ingredients; cover and process until smooth. Pour into chilled glasses; serve immediately.

CARAMEL CHIP MALTS

START TO FINISH: 5 MIN.
MAKES: 2 SERVINGS

- 1 **cup milk**
- 2 **cups chocolate chip ice cream**
- ½ **cup caramel ice cream topping**
- 3 **tablespoons chocolate malted milk powder**

In a blender, combine the milk, ice cream, caramel topping and chocolate malted milk powder; cover and process until blended. Pour into chilled glasses.

> Satisfy any sweet tooth in a hurry with a delicious chocolate chip malt that has a sweet hint of caramel. With its thick, creamy texture, it makes a speedy snack or dessert.
> —*TASTE OF HOME* TEST KITCHEN

CHOCOLATE ICE CREAM SODAS

I keep the ingredients for these ice cream sodas on hand so I can enjoy a treat any time I want. You can easily make more when feeding a crowd.
—**ANNA ERICKSON** SILVERDALE, WA

START TO FINISH: 15 MIN.
MAKES: 4 SERVINGS

- ¾ **cup chocolate syrup**
- 1 **cup milk**
- 4 **cups carbonated water, chilled**
- 8 **scoops chocolate ice cream (about 2⅔ cups), divided**
  Whipped cream in a can, optional

Place 3 tablespoons chocolate syrup in each of four 16-oz. glasses. Add ¼ cup milk and 1 cup carbonated water to each; stir until foamy. Add two scoops of ice cream to each glass. Top with whipped cream if desired.

WATERMELON SMOOTHIES

This is so good to sip on a hot day, and it's a snap to blend up.

—SANDI PICHON MEMPHIS, TN

START TO FINISH: 10 MIN.
MAKES: 6 SERVINGS

- 6 **cups coarsely chopped seedless watermelon**
- 1 **cup lemon sherbet**
- 12 **ice cubes**

Place half of the watermelon in a blender; cover and process until smooth. Add half of the sherbet and ice; cover and process until smooth. Repeat. Pour into chilled glasses; serve immediately.

COLA FLOATS

These thick, frosty floats add fun to any casual meal. Try substituting other soda and ice cream blends for the floats, like root beer with caramel-swirl ice cream.

—SHANNON ROUM ROCKFORD, IL

START TO FINISH: 5 MIN.
MAKES: 4 SERVINGS

- 4 **cups cherry cola, chilled**
- 1 **teaspoon vanilla extract**
- 8 **scoops fudge ripple ice cream**
  Whipped cream in a can, optional
- 4 **maraschino cherries**

In a pitcher, combine cola and vanilla. Place two scoops of ice cream in each of four chilled glasses. Pour cola over ice cream; top with whipped cream if desired and cherries.

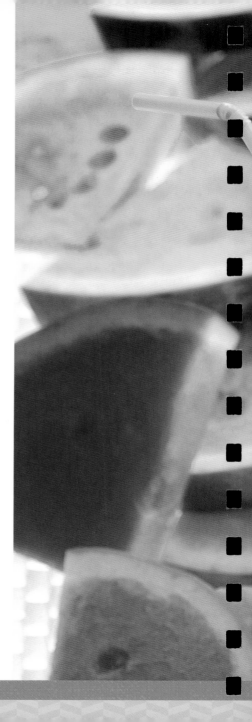

Watermelon
Smoothies

ORANGE SHERBET PARTY PUNCH

This punch is always a big hit with everyone. You can make the base for it several days ahead and chill. Before serving, add the sherbet and ginger ale.

—LANNIS BLUNK MASCOUTAH, IL

PREP: 15 MIN. + CHILLING
MAKES: 6½ QUARTS

- **4 cups water, divided**
- **1 package (6 ounces) strawberry gelatin**
- **1½ cups sugar**
- **1 can (46 ounces) pineapple juice**
- **1 can (46 ounces) orange juice**
- **1 cup lemon juice**
- **½ gallon orange sherbet, softened**
- **1 liter ginger ale, chilled**

1. Heat 2 cups water to boiling; add gelatin and sugar, stirring until dissolved. Add 2 cups cold water and fruit juices. Refrigerate until chilled.

2. Place mixture in a punch bowl; spoon in sherbet and pour in ginger ale. Serve immediately.

COOL LIME PIE FRAPPES

START TO FINISH: 10 MIN.
MAKES: 2 SERVINGS

- ¼ **cup fat-free milk**
- 2 **tablespoons lime juice**
- 2 **cups fat-free vanilla frozen yogurt, softened**
- ½ **teaspoon grated lime peel**
- 2 **teaspoons graham cracker crumbs**

In a blender, combine the milk, lime juice, frozen yogurt and lime peel; cover and process until blended. Stir if necessary. Pour into chilled glasses; sprinkle with cracker crumbs. Serve immediately.

> I love serving this light and luscious treat to guests on hot days. It has the taste and creamy texture of Key lime pie without the unwanted calories.
> —**MARIE RIZZIO** INTERLOCHEN, MI

NUTTY BANANA SHAKES

Kids of all ages will enjoy these thick shakes! Whip 'em up as a sweet and satisfying after-school snack, or sip them on the patio with a light lunch.
—**MARICAH LEVELLS** MEMPHIS, TN

START TO FINISH: 10 MIN.
MAKES: 5 SERVINGS

- 1 **cup milk**
- 3 **cups vanilla ice cream**
- 4 **medium ripe bananas, cut into chunks**
- ½ **cup chopped walnuts**
- 4 **miniature Butterfinger candy bars**

Place all ingredients in a blender; cover and process until blended. Pour into chilled glasses; serve immediately.

CARAMEL APPLE FLOATS

Who doesn't love the flavor of caramel, apples and vanilla ice cream? If I'm feeling fancy, I drizzle caramel syrup around the inside of the glasses before adding the apple cider and ginger ale.

—CINDY REAMS PHILIPSBURG, PA

START TO FINISH: 10 MIN. • **MAKES:** 2 SERVINGS

- 1 **cup chilled apple cider or unsweetened apple juice**
- 1 **cup chilled ginger ale or lemon-lime soda**
- 1 **cup vanilla ice cream**
- 2 **tablespoons caramel sundae syrup**

Divide cider and ginger ale between two glasses. Top with ice cream; drizzle with caramel syrup.

TANGY PARTY PUNCH

As social chair one year during college, I tried to come up with a more interesting beverage than the usual cranberry juice and lemon-lime soda. This pastel punch was always a hit at receptions and parties.

—JENNIFER BANGERTER NIXA, MO

START TO FINISH: 10 MIN. • **MAKES:** 8 QUARTS

- 1 **can (46 ounces) pineapple juice, chilled**
- 1 **can (46 ounces) orange juice, chilled**
- 1 **can (12 ounces) frozen limeade concentrate, thawed**
- 1 **can (12 ounces) frozen lemonade concentrate, thawed**
- 3 **liters ginger ale, chilled**
- 1 **pint each orange, lemon and lime sherbet**

In a punch bowl, combine the first four ingredients. Stir in ginger ale. Add scoops of sherbet. Serve immediately.

Caramel Apple Floats

Peanut Butter
Milk Shakes

PEANUT BUTTER MILK SHAKES

START TO FINISH: 5 MIN. • **MAKES:** 3 SERVINGS

- 1 **cup milk**
- 2 **cups vanilla ice cream**
- ½ **cup peanut butter**
- 2 **tablespoons sugar**

In a blender, combine all ingredients; cover and process for 30 seconds or until smooth. Stir if necessary. Pour into chilled glasses; serve immediately.

> You've got milk. You've got peanut butter. Probably vanilla ice cream, too. With just a few everyday ingredients, you can whip up these creamy treats in a couple of minutes.
> —**JOYCE TURLEY** SLAUGHTERS, KY

DIY
ICE CREAM

GEORGIA PEACH ICE CREAM

Georgia is well known for its state fruit, and blending tree-ripened peaches into homemade ice cream is heavenly. This Southern treat has been a favorite in our family for more than 50 years.

—MARGUERITE ETHRIDGE AMERICUS, GA

PREP: 45 MIN. + CHILLING
PROCESS: 20 MIN./BATCH + FREEZING
MAKES: 3¾ QUARTS

- 4 **eggs**
- 1¼ **cups sugar, divided**
- ½ **teaspoon salt**
- 4 **cups whole milk**
- 2 **cans (14 ounces each) sweetened condensed milk**
- 1¾ **pounds fresh peaches, peeled and sliced**

1. In a large heavy saucepan, whisk eggs, 1 cup sugar and salt until blended; stir in milk. Cook over low heat until mixture is just thick enough to coat a spoon and a thermometer reads at least 160°, stirring constantly. Do not allow to boil. Remove from heat immediately.

2. Quickly transfer to a bowl; place the bowl in a pan of ice water. Stir gently and occasionally for 2 minutes. Stir in the sweetened condensed milk. Press plastic wrap onto the surface of the custard. Refrigerate several hours or overnight.

3. When ready to freeze, in a small bowl, mash the peaches with the remaining sugar; let stand 30 minutes. Fill the cylinder of ice cream freezer two-thirds full with custard, stirring in some of the peaches; freeze according to manufacturer's directions. Refrigerate remaining mixture until ready to freeze.

4. Transfer ice cream to freezer containers, allowing headspace for expansion. Freeze 2-4 hours or until firm. Repeat with remaining ice cream mixture and peaches.

CHOCOLATE CRUNCH ICE CREAM

The delightful crunch in this decadent ice cream comes from chunks of chocolate, toffee bits and slivered almonds. I toast the nuts in advance and separate all my add-ins into labeled containers.

—ROSALIE PETERS CALDWELL, TX

PREP: 30 MIN. + CHILLING
PROCESS: 20 MIN./BATCH + FREEZING
MAKES: 1½ QUARTS

- 1½ **cups milk**
- ¾ **cup sugar, divided**
- 4 **egg yolks**
- 2½ **teaspoons instant coffee granules**
- 2 **cups 60% cacao bittersweet chocolate baking chips, melted and cooled**
- 1½ **cups heavy whipping cream**
- 1 **teaspoon vanilla extract**
- ¾ **cup semisweet chocolate chips, melted**
- ¾ **cup slivered almonds, toasted**
- ⅓ **cup milk chocolate toffee bits**

1. In a large saucepan, heat the milk to 175°; stir in ½ cup sugar until dissolved. In a small bowl, whisk the egg yolks and remaining sugar. Stir in coffee granules and bittersweet chocolate.

2. In small bowl, whisk a small amount of the hot mixture into the egg yolks; return all to pan, whisking constantly. Cook over low heat until the mixture is just thick enough to coat a metal spoon and a thermometer reads at least 160°, stirring constantly. Do not allow to boil. Remove from heat immediately.

3. Quickly transfer to a large bowl; place the bowl in a pan of ice water. Stir gently and occasionally for 2 minutes. Stir in cream and vanilla. Press plastic wrap onto the surface of the custard. Refrigerate several hours or overnight.

4. Line a baking sheet with waxed paper; spread the melted semisweet chocolate chips to ⅛-in. thickness. Refrigerate chocolate for 20 minutes; chop coarsely.

5. Fill cylinder of ice cream freezer two-thirds full with custard; freeze according to manufacturer's directions. (Refrigerate any remaining mixture until ready to freeze.)

6. Transfer the ice cream to freezer containers, allowing headspace for expansion. For each batch, stir in some of the chopped chocolate, almonds and chocolate toffee bits. Freeze 2-4 hours or until firm.

TOASTING NUTS

Spread nuts in a 15x10x1-in. baking pan. Bake at 350° for 5-10 minutes or until lightly browned, stirring occasionally.

CITRUS-MELON SORBET

My mother made her citrus-cantaloupe sorbet all the time in summer. You can substitute different types of fruit—all you need is a blender or a food processor.
—PATRICIA HANCOCK HAWTHORNE, NJ

PREP: 15 MIN. + FREEZING
MAKES: 2 CUPS

- ¼ **cup orange juice**
- 2 **tablespoons lime juice**
- 3 **cups diced cantaloupe**
- ¾ **cup sugar**
- 1 **teaspoon grated lemon peel**
- 1 **teaspoon grated lime peel**

1. In a blender, combine all ingredients. Cover and process 1-2 minutes or until smooth. Transfer puree to a 13x9x2-in. dish. Cover and freeze 45 minutes or until the edges begin to firm; stir.
2. Freeze 2 hours longer or until firm. Just before serving, transfer to a blender; cover and process 2-3 minutes or until smooth.

Cranberry
Buttermilk Sherbet

CRANBERRY BUTTERMILK SHERBET

PREP: 25 MIN.
PROCESS: 20 MIN. + FREEZING
MAKES: ABOUT 1 QUART

- **1 cup fresh or frozen cranberries**
- **¼ cup packed brown sugar**
- **¼ cup orange juice**
- **½ teaspoon grated lemon peel**
- **½ teaspoon grated orange peel**
- **1 cinnamon stick (3 inches)**
- **2 cups buttermilk**
- **1 cup sugar**
- **1 cup light corn syrup**
- **¼ cup lemon juice**
- **Dash salt**

1. In a small saucepan, combine first six ingredients; cook over medium heat until the berries pop, about 15 minutes. Discard the cinnamon stick. Mash the cranberry mixture; chill.

1. In a large bowl, combine buttermilk, sugar, light corn syrup, lemon juice and salt; add the cranberry mixture. Pour into the cylinder of ice cream freezer; freeze according to the manufacturer's directions. Transfer the ice cream to freezer containers, allowing headspace for expansion. Freeze 2-4 hours or until firm.

> This refreshing cranberry sherbet is a great counterpoint to rich holiday foods, but you'll want to enjoy it year-round. The buttermilk adds a wonderful tang.
> —**LISA SPEER** PALM BEACH, FL

FROSTY NOTES

_____
_____
_____
_____
_____
_____
_____
_____
_____
_____
_____
_____
_____
_____
_____
_____
_____
_____
_____
_____
_____
_____
_____
_____
_____
_____
_____
_____
_____
_____
_____
_____
_____
_____
_____
_____

PEANUT BUTTER CHEESECAKE ICE CREAM

Want something frosty but decadent for a party or holiday feast? Serve generous slices of a freezer cheesecake dessert featuring chopped peanuts, cookies and drizzled toppings. Yum!

—TERRYANN MOORE VINELAND, NJ

PREP: 35 MIN. + FREEZING • **MAKES:** 16 SERVINGS

- 2 **cups whole milk**
- 1½ **cups packed brown sugar**
- 2 **packages (8 ounces each) cream cheese, softened**
- 1 **cup creamy peanut butter**
- 1½ **cups heavy whipping cream**
- 3 **teaspoons vanilla extract**
- 24 **Oreo cookies, coarsely chopped**
- 1 **cup coarsely chopped salted peanuts**
  Chocolate and caramel ice cream topping
  Whipped cream, optional

1. In a small saucepan, combine the milk and brown sugar; cook and stir over medium heat until the brown sugar is dissolved. Cool to room temperature.

2. In a large bowl, beat the cream cheese and peanut butter until blended. Gradually add milk mixture, cream and vanilla; beat until smooth. Press plastic wrap onto the surface of mixture. Refrigerate several hours or overnight.

3. Pour half of the cream cheese mixture into cylinder of ice cream freezer; freeze according to manufacturer's directions, adding half of the chopped cookies and half of the peanuts during the last 2 minutes of processing. (Refrigerate the remaining mixture until ready to freeze.) Transfer ice cream to a 9-in. springform pan.

4. Repeat with the remaining cream cheese mixture, cookies and peanuts. Transfer to the pan. Freeze until firm, about 4 hours.

5. To serve, remove rim from pan. Drizzle ice cream with chocolate and caramel toppings. If desired, serve with whipped cream.

Peanut Butter
Cheesecake Ice Cream

1. Place strawberries, raspberries, sugar and juices in a blender. Cover and process for 2-3 minutes or until smooth. Transfer to a 13x9x2-in. dish. Freeze 1 hour or until the edges begin to firm.

2. Stir and return to freezer. Freeze 2 hours longer or until firm.

3. Just before serving, transfer to a food processor; cover and process 2-3 minutes or until smooth. Garnish each serving with fresh raspberries and lime wedges if desired.

MOTHER'S BANANA SHERBET

Smooth, citrusy banana sherbet is so popular with my family, I usually triple the recipe. And even then, it's not enough!
—**KATHY BARTON** HOMER, MI

PREP: 15 MIN.
PROCESS: 20 MIN. + FREEZING
MAKES: 2½ CUPS

- 1 **cup water**
- ⅔ **cup sugar**
- ⅓ **cup reduced-fat evaporated milk**
- ⅓ **cup orange juice**
- 2 **tablespoons lemon juice**
- 1 **medium banana, cut into chunks**

1. In a small saucepan, bring the water and sugar to a boil. Cook and stir until sugar is dissolved; set aside to cool.

2. Place the evaporated milk, orange juice, lemon juice and banana in a blender. Add the sugar syrup; cover and process until smooth.

3. Pour mixture into the cylinder of ice cream freezer; freeze according to the manufacturer's directions. Transfer to a freezer container, allowing headspace for expansion. Freeze for 4 hours or until firm before serving.

STRAWBERRY-RASPBERRY ICE

With its ruby-red color and summery taste, this frosty delight is irresistible on a hot day. Feel free to use any canned fruit in place of the strawberries and raspberries—just be sure to freeze the can first.
—**SANDRA SAKAITIS** ST. LOUIS, MO

PREP: 10 MIN. + FREEZING
MAKES: 3½ CUPS

- 2 **packages (10 ounces each) frozen sweetened sliced strawberries, partially thawed**
- 2 **cups frozen unsweetened raspberries, partially thawed**
- ⅓ **cup sugar**
- 3 **tablespoons lime juice**
- 2 **tablespoons orange juice**
  Fresh raspberries and lime wedges, optional

FROZEN STRAWBERRY YOGURT

After losing 60 pounds, I wanted to find a lighter dessert. Even people who aren't watching their diet like this frozen yogurt.
—**TERI VAN WEY** SALINA, KS

PREP: 15 MIN. + FREEZING
MAKES: 1½ QUARTS

- **2 cups (16 ounces) fat-free plain yogurt**
- **2 cups pureed fresh strawberries**
- **1 can (14 ounces) fat-free sweetened condensed milk**
- **1 cup fat-free milk**
- **3 teaspoons vanilla extract**

1. In a large bowl, combine all the ingredients. Fill the cylinder of ice cream freezer two-thirds full; freeze according to manufacturer's directions. (Refrigerate any remaining mixture until ready to freeze.) Transfer the ice cream to freezer containers, allowing headspace for expansion. Freeze 2-4 hours or until firm. Repeat with any remaining ice cream mixture.
2. Remove from freezer 30-45 minutes before serving.

ROCKY ROAD ICE CREAM

When it comes to ice cream, my daughters clamor for rocky road. Sometimes we add extra chips on top and whipped cream, too.
—**DALE LANGFORD** ATWATER, CA

PREP: 15 MIN. + COOLING
PROCESS: 20 MIN./BATCH + FREEZING
MAKES: ABOUT 4½ QUARTS

- **3 cups whole milk**
- **3 cups half-and-half cream**
- **9 ounces semisweet chocolate, chopped**
- **2¾ cups sugar**
- **¾ teaspoon salt**
- **6 cups heavy whipping cream**
- **3 cups miniature marshmallows**
- **2¼ cups miniature semisweet chocolate chips**
- **1½ cups chopped pecans**
- **6 teaspoons vanilla extract**

1. In a large saucepan, combine the milk and half-and-half; heat to 175°. Add the chocolate, sugar and salt; stir until chocolate is melted and sugar is dissolved. Remove from heat.
2. Quickly transfer to a large bowl; place bowl in a pan of ice water. Stir gently and occasionally for 2 minutes. Stir in remaining ingredients. Press plastic wrap onto surface of custard. Cover and refrigerate for 30 minutes.
3. Fill cylinder of ice cream freezer two-thirds full; freeze according to the manufacturer's directions. (Refrigerate remaining mixture until ready to freeze.) Transfer ice cream to freezer containers, allowing headspace for expansion. Freeze 2-4 hours or until firm. Repeat with remaining ice cream mixture.

Apricot Lemon Ice

APRICOT LEMON ICE

This sunny favorite is guaranteed to melt any resistance to dessert! The recipe is a great choice for friends or relatives who are lactose intolerant. And with only five simple ingredients, it couldn't be easier to make.

—**ELIZABETH MONTGOMERY** ALLSTON, MA

PREP: 15 MIN. + FREEZING
MAKES: 6 SERVINGS

- 1 envelope unflavored gelatin
- ½ cup cold water
- 3 cups apricot nectar
- ½ cup light corn syrup
- ¼ cup lemon juice

1. In a small saucepan, sprinkle the unflavored gelatin over the cold water; let stand 1 minute. Cook over low heat, stirring until the gelatin is completely dissolved. Remove from the heat; stir in the apricot nectar, light corn syrup and lemon juice.

2. Pour into a shallow dish. Cover and freeze 2-3 hours or until firm.

3. Spoon mixture into a large chilled metal bowl; beat 1-2 minutes or until light and creamy. Return to shallow container. Cover and freeze until firm.

BANANA SPLIT ICE CREAM

I love experimenting with ice cream recipes and coming up with my own concoctions. Here's a lower-fat creation that features the yummy ingredients of a banana split.

—**CAROL DALE** GREENVILLE, TX

PREP: 20 MIN. + CHILLING
PROCESS: 20 MIN./BATCH + FREEZING
MAKES: ABOUT 2½ QUARTS

- 5 cups fat-free milk, divided
- 1 cup egg substitute
- 2 cans (14 ounces each) fat-free sweetened condensed milk
- 2 medium ripe bananas, mashed
- 2 tablespoons lime juice
- 1 tablespoon vanilla extract
- ¾ cup fat-free chocolate ice cream topping
- ½ cup chopped pecans
- ¼ cup chopped maraschino cherries

1. In a heavy saucepan, combine 2½ cups fat-free milk and the egg substitute. Cook over low heat until the mixture is thick enough to coat a metal spoon and reaches at least 160°, stirring constantly. Do not allow to boil. Remove from heat immediately.

2. Quickly transfer to a large bowl; place bowl in a pan of ice water. Stir gently and occasionally for 2 minutes. Stir in condensed milk and remaining fat-free milk. Press plastic wrap onto surface of custard. Refrigerate several hours or overnight.

3. Combine bananas, lime juice and vanilla; stir into custard mixture. Fill ice cream freezer two-thirds full; freeze according to manufacturer's directions. (Refrigerate remaining mixture until ready to freeze.) Transfer ice cream to freezer containers, allowing headspace for expansion; gently fold in chocolate topping, pecans and cherries. Freeze 2-4 hours or until firm.

GO BANANAS

If bananas are too green, place them in a paper bag until ripe. Adding an apple to the bag will speed up the process. Store ripe bananas at room temperature.

LOW-FAT VANILLA ICE CREAM

Is vanilla your flavor? Scoop up a guilt-free version that has all the goodness you crave.
—**REBECCA BAIRD** SALT LAKE CITY, UT

PREP: 20 MIN. + CHILLING
PROCESS: 20 MIN./BATCH + FREEZING
MAKES: 1 QUART

- ¾ **cup sugar**
- 3 **tablespoons cornstarch**
- ⅛ **teaspoon salt**
- 4 **cups fat-free half-and-half**
- 2 **egg yolks, beaten**
- 3 **teaspoons vanilla extract**

1. In a large saucepan, combine the sugar, cornstarch and salt. Gradually add half-and-half; stir until smooth. Bring to a boil over medium heat; cook and stir 2 minutes or until thickened. Remove from heat.
2. In a small bowl, whisk a small amount of the hot mixture into egg yolks; return all to the pan, whisking constantly. Bring to a gentle boil; cook and stir 2 minutes. Remove from heat. Stir in vanilla.
3. Quickly transfer to a large bowl; place bowl in a pan of ice water. Stir gently and occasionally for 2 minutes. Press plastic wrap onto the surface of the custard. Refrigerate several hours or overnight.
4. Fill the cylinder of ice cream maker two-thirds full; freeze according to the manufacturer's directions. Transfer the ice cream to freezer containers, allowing headspace for expansion. Freeze 2-4 hours or until firm.

EASY MINT CHIP ICE CREAM

Yes, you *can* make ice cream without using special equipment! Just combine a handful of readily available ingredients and pour the mixture into a standard-size loaf pan. Pop it into the freezer to set up overnight, and presto—a mint chocolate chip delight. Dish out bowlfuls and wait for the smiles!
—**CYNTHIA KOLBERG** SYRACUSE, IN

PREP: 15 MIN. + FREEZING
MAKES: 8 SERVINGS

- 1 **can (14 ounces) sweetened condensed milk**
- 2 **tablespoons water**
- ¼ **to ½ teaspoon peppermint extract**
- 3 **to 4 drops green food coloring**
- 2 **cups heavy whipping cream, whipped**
- 1 **cup (6 ounces) miniature semisweet chocolate chips**

In a large bowl, combine milk, water, extract and food coloring. Fold in the whipped cream and chocolate chips. Pour into a foil-lined 9x5-in. loaf pan. Cover and freeze 6 hours or until firm. Lift out of the pan and remove foil; slice.

STRAWBERRY MANGO SORBET

What a way to enjoy fresh-picked summer strawberries! Combining them with yummy mangoes adds a tropical twist.

—SANDRA VACHON SAINT-CONSTANT, QC

PREP: 20 MIN. + FREEZING
MAKES: 1 QUART

- ¾ **cup sugar**
- 1½ **cups water**
- 1½ **cups chopped peeled mangoes**
- 1½ **cups fresh strawberries, halved**
- ¼ **cup lime juice**

1. In a small saucepan, bring the sugar and water to a boil. Cook and stir until sugar is dissolved; set aside to cool.

2. Place the mangoes and strawberries in a food processor; add the sugar syrup and lime juice. Cover and process until pureed. Transfer puree to a 13x9x2-in. dish. Freeze 45 minutes or until the edges begin to firm. Stir and return to the freezer. Freeze 2 hours longer or until firm.

3. Just before serving, transfer to a food processor; cover and process 2-3 minutes or until smooth.

Lemon Plum Sorbet

LEMON PLUM SORBET

PREP: 25 MIN. + FREEZING • **MAKES:** 6 SERVINGS

- 8 **medium plums**
- 2 **cups sugar**
- 1 **cup water**
- ⅓ **cup lemon juice**
- 2 **teaspoons grated lemon peel**

1. In a large saucepan, bring 8 cups water to a boil. Add plums; cover and boil for 30-45 seconds. Drain and immediately place plums in ice water. Drain and pat dry. When cool enough to handle, remove skins. Cut in half; remove pits.

2. In a small saucepan, bring sugar and 1 cup water to a boil. Cook and stir until the sugar is dissolved. Add the lemon juice and lemon peel; set aside to cool.

3. Place the plums in a food processor; add sugar syrup. Cover and process for 2-3 minutes or until smooth. Transfer puree to an 8-in.- square dish. Freeze for 1 hour or until edges begin to firm; stir. Freeze 2 hours longer or until firm.

4. Just before serving, transfer the sorbet to a food processor; cover and process for 2-3 minutes or until smooth.

> Lemon and plums make a wonderfully refreshing pair in this pretty sorbet. Enjoy it plain or add a scoop to a slice of angel food cake.
> —**EIRIANEDD SIMPSON** PAHRUMP, NV

APPLE TARRAGON GRANITA

Here's a delightfully different take on classic Italian granita. Fresh tarragon complements the bright, sweet apple flavor.

—DEBBY HARDEN WILLIAMSTON, MI

PREP: 10 MIN. + FREEZING
MAKES: 6 SERVINGS

- **3 cups unsweetened apple juice**
- **½ cup sugar**
- **2 tablespoons coarsely chopped fresh tarragon**
- **4 teaspoons lemon juice**

1. In an 8-in.-square dish, combine all ingredients until the sugar is dissolved. Freeze 1 hour; stir with a fork. Freeze 2-3 hours longer or until completely frozen, stirring every 30 minutes.

2. Stir granita with a fork just before serving; spoon into dessert dishes.

PINEAPPLE BUTTERMILK SHERBET

Just canned pineapple, buttermilk and sugar go into this irresistible sherbet.

—DOLORES KASTELLO WAUKESHA, WI

PREP: 10 MIN. + FREEZING
MAKES: 1¼ QUARTS

- **1 can (20 ounces) unsweetened crushed pineapple, undrained**
- **2 cups buttermilk**
- **¾ cup sugar**

1. In a large bowl, combine all ingredients; stir until the sugar is dissolved. Pour into an 8-in.-square dish. Cover and freeze 1 to 1½ hours or until mixture begins to harden.

2. Stir the mixture; freeze 3-4 hours longer or until firm, stirring occasionally. To use sherbet, remove from the freezer 20 minutes before serving.

Apple Tarragon Granita

TRY TARRAGON

Tarragon is an herb with slender green leaves and a distinctive anise-like flavor. It is widely used in French cooking and goes well with chicken, fish and vegetable dishes. It's best known for flavoring Bearnaise sauce and for making flavored vinegar.

PEACH ICE

Making dinner for just the two of you? Surprise that special someone with an icy, perfect-for-a-pair dessert. For extra flair, garnish each serving with slices of fresh peaches and a sprig of mint.

—CARMA BLOSSER LIVERMORE, CO

PREP: 15 MIN. + FREEZING
MAKES: 2 SERVINGS

- ⅓ **cup warm water (120° to 130°)**
- 2 **tablespoons sugar**
- 1 **small peach, peeled**
- 2 **teaspoons lemon juice**

1. In a small bowl, stir water and sugar until sugar is dissolved. Place peach, lemon juice and sugar mixture in a blender. Cover and process 1 minute or until blended. Transfer to a freezer container; cover and freeze 3 hours or until almost firm.

2. Transfer to blender. Cover and process 30-40 seconds or until slushy. Return to freezer container; cover and freeze overnight.

3. Remove from freezer just before serving. Using a fork, scrape into two dessert dishes.

COOKIE DOUGH ICE CREAM

My grandmother's chocolate chip cookie dough cheesecake is so good, I was inspired to turn it into an ice cream. Divine!
—STACIE WASH CHESTERFIELD, VA

PREP: 30 MIN. + CHILLING
PROCESS: 20 MIN./BATCH + FREEZING
MAKES: 2 QUARTS

- ¾ **to 1 cup refrigerated chocolate chip cookie dough**

CRUST
- 2 **cups chocolate graham cracker crumbs (about 26 squares)**
- 2 **tablespoons sugar**
- ½ **cup butter, melted**

ICE CREAM
- 2 **cups half-and-half cream**
- 1 **cup sugar**
- 2 **cups heavy whipping cream**
- 6 **teaspoons vanilla extract**
- 12 **ounces cream cheese, softened and cubed**

1. Pinch off small pieces of the cookie dough; place on a greased baking sheet. Cover and freeze.
2. Meanwhile, preheat oven to 350°. In a bowl, combine the cracker crumbs and sugar; stir in butter. Press into a greased 15x10x1-in. baking pan. Bake 11-15 minutes or until set. Cool on a wire rack. Break into small pieces; set aside.
3. For ice cream, in a small saucepan, heat half-and-half to 175°; stir in sugar until dissolved. Remove from heat. Cool quickly by placing pan in a bowl of ice water; stir for 2 minutes. Pour into a large bowl.
4. In a blender, combine cream, vanilla and cream cheese; cover and process until smooth. Stir into half-and-half mixture. Cover and refrigerate for several hours or overnight.

5. Fill cylinder of ice cream freezer two-thirds full; freeze according to the manufacturer's directions (the mixture will be very soft). (Refrigerate remaining mixture until ready to freeze.)
6. For each batch, in a large bowl, layer a third of ice cream, some of dough and crust pieces; repeat layers twice. Swirl ice cream. Freeze 2-4 hours before serving.
NOTE *For food safety reasons, use only commercially prepared cookie dough.*

BLACK CHERRY SHERBET

Sometimes I prepare this recipe using a sugar substitute—it works just as well.
—EMILY EVANS ROSELLE, IL

PREP: 25 MIN. + CHILLING
PROCESS: 20 MIN./BATCH + FREEZING
MAKES: 2½ QUARTS

- 4 **cups fresh or frozen quartered pitted dark sweet cherries, thawed**
- 1 **cup sugar**
- 2 **liters black cherry soda, chilled**
- 1 **can (14 ounces) sweetened condensed milk**
- 1 **cup (6 ounces) miniature semisweet chocolate chips**

1. In a large saucepan over medium heat, cook the cherries and sugar for 15 minutes or until slightly thickened, stirring occasionally. Transfer to a large bowl; cool to room temperature. Refrigerate until chilled.
2. Stir in the soda, milk and chips. Fill cylinder of ice cream freezer two-thirds full; freeze according to manufacturer's directions. (Refrigerate the remaining mixture until ready to freeze.) Transfer the ice cream to freezer containers, allowing headspace for expansion. Freeze 2-4 hours or until firm. Repeat with remaining ice cream mixture.

GRANDMA'S ORANGE MILK SHERBET

When I was a child, my dear grandma made this citrusy sherbet for my birthday party. She squeezed whole oranges to get the juice for it. I frequently double the recipe because everyone wants a scoop.

—MARILYNN ENGELBRECHT

HARRISONVILLE, MO

PREP: 20 MIN. + FREEZING
MAKES: ABOUT 2 QUARTS

- 3 **cups milk**
- 1½ **cups orange juice**
- ¾ **cup sugar**
- 2 **cans (8 ounces each) unsweetened crushed pineapple**

1. In a large saucepan, heat the milk over medium heat until bubbles form around sides of pan. Set aside to cool.
2. In a large bowl, combine the orange juice and sugar thoroughly. Stir in the milk. Transfer to an 11x7-in. dish; freeze until mushy.
3. Transfer the mixture to a bowl and whip. Add pineapple and juices. Return to dish and freeze.

BANANA CITRUS SORBET

A friend who loves to entertain gave me the recipe for this delightful sorbet. Serving it as a refreshing special course adds a bit of elegance to my favorite meal. If you don't have an ice cream freezer, put the mixture into ice cube trays and stir it occasionally while freezing. Then simply mix it in a blender when you're ready to serve.

—MILLIE VICKERY LENA, IL

PREP: 10 MIN.
PROCESS: 20 MIN./BATCH + FREEZING
MAKES: 2½ QUARTS

- ½ **cup lemon juice**
- 3 **medium ripe bananas, cut into chunks**
- 1½ **cups sugar**
- 2 **cups cold water**
- 1½ **cups orange juice**

1. Place lemon juice and bananas in blender; cover and process until smooth. Add sugar; cover and process until blended. Transfer to a large bowl; stir in water and orange juice.
2. Fill cylinder of ice cream freezer two-thirds full; freeze according to the manufacturer's directions. (Refrigerate the remaining mixture until ready to freeze.) Transfer to a freezer container, allowing headspace for expansion. Freeze 2-4 hours before serving. Repeat with remaining sorbet mixture. May be frozen up to 1 month.

WATERMELON BERRY SORBET

Strawberries, watermelon and three other items are all you need for this freezer treat that's virtually free of fat. It's the ultimate in summertime desserts.

—JILL SWAVELY GREEN LANE, PA

PREP: 30 MIN. + FREEZING
MAKES: 6 SERVINGS

- 1 **cup water**
- ½ **cup sugar**
- 2 **cups cubed seedless watermelon**
- 2 **cups fresh strawberries, hulled**
- 1 **tablespoon minced fresh mint**

1. In a small heavy saucepan, bring water and sugar to a boil. Cook and stir until the sugar is dissolved. Remove from heat; cool slightly.

2. Place the cubed watermelon and strawberries in a blender; add sugar syrup. Cover and process 2-3 minutes or until smooth. Strain and discard seeds and pulp. Transfer puree to a 13x9x2-in. dish. Freeze 1 hour or until edges begin to firm. Stir in mint. Freeze 2 hours longer or until firm.

3. Just before serving, transfer to a blender; cover and process 2-3 minutes or until smooth.

Chunky Banana
Cream Freeze

CHUNKY BANANA CREAM FREEZE

A medley of banana, almond, coconut and peanut butter flavors, this treat is loaded with walnuts and raisins for good measure!
—**KRISTEN BLOOM** APO, AP

PREP: 15 MIN. + FREEZING
MAKES: 3 CUPS

- 5 **medium bananas, peeled and frozen**
- ⅓ **cup almond milk**
- 2 **tablespoons finely shredded unsweetened coconut**
- 2 **tablespoons creamy peanut butter**
- 1 **teaspoon vanilla extract**
- ¼ **cup chopped walnuts**
- 3 **tablespoons raisins**

1. Place the bananas, almond milk, coconut, peanut butter and vanilla in a food processor; cover and process until blended.
2. Transfer to a freezer container; stir in the walnuts and raisins. Freeze for 2-4 hours before serving.
NOTE *Look for unsweetened coconut in the baking or health food section.*

OLD-FASHIONED STRAWBERRY ICE CREAM

Our state produces a lot of strawberries, and I love using them for ice cream.
—**LEONE MAYNE** FROSTPROOF, FL

PREP: 30 MIN. + CHILLING
PROCESS: 20 MIN. + FREEZING
MAKES: ABOUT 2 QUARTS

- 2 **eggs**
- 2 **cups milk**
- 1¼ **cups sugar**
- 1 **cup miniature marshmallows**
- 2 **cups pureed strawberries**
- 1 **cup half-and-half cream**
- ½ **cup heavy whipping cream**
- 1 **teaspoon vanilla extract**

1. In a large heavy saucepan, combine the eggs and milk; stir in sugar. Cook over low heat until the mixture is just thick enough to coat a metal spoon and a thermometer reads at least 160°, stirring constantly. Do not allow to boil. Remove from heat immediately; add marshmallows, stirring until melted.
2. Quickly transfer to a large bowl; place the bowl in a pan of ice water. Stir gently and occasionally for 5-10 minutes or until cool. Stir in the remaining ingredients. Press plastic wrap onto surface of custard. Refrigerate several hours or overnight.
3. Fill cylinder of ice cream freezer two-thirds full; freeze according to the manufacturer's directions. (Refrigerate the remaining mixture until ready to freeze.) Transfer ice cream to freezer containers, allowing headspace for expansion. Freeze 2-4 hours or until firm. Repeat with the remaining ice cream mixture.

PRALINE CRUNCH ICE CREAM

If you're a caramel lover, you'll want to try my homemade ice cream sprinkled with crunchy candied pecans and drizzled with a rich caramel sauce. I've used this recipe for ice cream socials at our church, and I always get compliments.

—JULIA REGISTER HUNTERSVILLE, NC

PREP: 30 MIN. + CHILLING
PROCESS: 20 MIN./BATCH + FREEZING
MAKES: ABOUT 1½ QUARTS ICE CREAM (1½ CUPS SAUCE)

- 1¾ **cups milk**
- ⅔ **cup sugar**
- 2 **eggs, beaten**
- 2 **cups heavy whipping cream**
- 1 **teaspoon vanilla extract**

CANDIED PECANS

- 1 **tablespoon butter**
- ¼ **cup packed brown sugar**
- ¼ **teaspoon ground cinnamon**
  Dash ground nutmeg
- ½ **cup chopped pecans**

CARAMEL SAUCE

- 1 **cup butter, cubed**
- ½ **cup water**
- 1 **tablespoon light corn syrup**
- 2 **cups sugar**
- 1 **cup heavy whipping cream**

1. In a heavy saucepan, heat the milk to 175°; stir in the sugar until dissolved. Whisk a small amount of hot mixture into eggs; return all to the pan, whisking constantly. Cook over low heat until the mixture is just thick enough to coat a metal spoon and a thermometer reads at least 160°, stirring constantly. Do not allow to boil. Remove from the heat immediately.

2. Quickly transfer to a large bowl; place bowl in a pan of ice water. Stir gently and occasionally for 2 minutes. Stir in cream and vanilla. Press plastic wrap onto the surface of the custard. Refrigerate several hours or overnight.

3. Fill cylinder of ice cream freezer two-thirds full; freeze according to the manufacturer's directions. (Refrigerate any remaining mixture until ready to freeze.) Transfer ice cream to freezer containers, allowing headspace for expansion. Freeze 2-4 hours or until firm. Repeat with any remaining ice cream mixture.

4. In a heavy skillet, melt butter over medium heat. Stir in the brown sugar, cinnamon and nutmeg; cook and stir until sugar is dissolved. Add pecans; cook and stir 2-3 minutes or until coated. Spread pecans onto a greased foil-lined baking sheet. Cool completely.

5. For sauce, combine butter, water and corn syrup in a heavy saucepan. Cook and stir over medium-low heat until the butter is melted. Add sugar; cook and stir until sugar is dissolved. Bring to a boil over medium-high heat without stirring. Boil 4 minutes. Stir 6-8 minutes or until the mixture is caramel-colored. Remove from heat. Carefully stir in cream until smooth. Serve caramel sauce and candied pecans over ice cream.

PEPPERMINT ICE CREAM

Bits of crushed peppermint candy are perfect for the Christmas holiday season.

—BERNEICE METCALF LEAVENWORTH, WA

PREP: 15 MIN. + CHILLING
PROCESS: 20 MIN./BATCH + FREEZING
MAKES: 1 QUART

- 1½ **cups half-and-half cream**
- ¾ **cup sugar**
- ¼ **teaspoon salt**
- 4 **egg yolks**
- 2 **cups heavy whipping cream**
- 4½ **to 6 teaspoons vanilla extract**
- 1 **to 1¼ cups crushed peppermint candy**

1. In a large saucepan, heat half-and-half to 175°; stir in sugar and salt until dissolved. Whisk a small amount of the hot mixture into yolks. Return all to the pan, whisking constantly. Cook over low heat until mixture is just thick enough to coat a metal spoon and a thermometer reads at least 160°, stirring constantly. Do not allow to boil. Remove from the heat immediately.

2. Quickly transfer to a large bowl; place bowl in a pan of ice water. Stir gently and occasionally for 2 minutes. Stir in the cream and vanilla. Press plastic wrap onto surface of custard. Refrigerate several hours or overnight.

3. Fill cylinder of ice cream freezer two-thirds full; freeze according to the manufacturer's directions. (Refrigerate any remaining mixture until ready to freeze.) Transfer ice cream to freezer containers, allowing headspace for expansion. For each batch, stir in some of the peppermint candy. Freeze 2-4 hours or until firm.

STRAWBERRY ICE CREAM

When it's warm out, we dig into this cool treat. But we always find reasons to make it when the weather's cold, too!

—**KIMBERLEY WHITHAM** MOSCOW, KS

PREP: 1 HOUR + COOLING
PROCESS: 20 MIN. + FREEZING
MAKES: 3 QUARTS

- 6 **tablespoons all-purpose flour**
- 3 **cups sugar, divided**
- 1 **teaspoon salt**
- 4 **cups milk**
- 6 **eggs**
- 1½ **pints strawberries, hulled**
- 2 **tablespoons lemon juice**
- 4 **cups half-and-half cream**
- 2 **tablespoons vanilla extract**
  Red food coloring

1. In a large saucepan, combine flour, 2 cups sugar and salt. Whisk in milk. Cook and stir over medium heat until thickened and bubbly. Reduce heat to low; cook and stir 2 minutes longer. Remove from heat.
2. In a large bowl, whisk a small amount of hot mixture into eggs; return all to pan, whisking constantly. Bring to a gentle boil; cook and stir 2 minutes. Remove from heat immediately.
3. Quickly transfer to a large bowl; place the bowl in a pan of ice water. Stir gently and occasionally for 2 minutes. Press plastic wrap onto surface of custard. Refrigerate several hours or overnight.
4. Meanwhile, in a medium bowl and using a potato masher, crush berries with lemon juice and remaining sugar. Let stand 1 hour. Stir the cream, vanilla, red food coloring if desired and berry mixture into custard.
5. Fill cylinder of ice cream freezer two-thirds full; freeze according to the manufacturer's directions. (Refrigerate the remaining mixture until ready to freeze.) Transfer ice cream to freezer containers, allowing headspace for expansion. Freeze 2-4 hours or until firm. Repeat with the remaining ice cream mixture.

SOUR CHERRY SORBET

The fruit from my mother-in-law's cherry tree is so good in a sweet-tart sorbet.

—**CAROL GAUS** ELK GROVE VILLAGE, IL

PREP: 10 MIN. + FREEZING
MAKES: 6 SERVINGS

- 3 **cups frozen pitted tart cherries**
- 1 **cup sugar**
- ⅓ **cup white wine or grape juice**
- ½ **teaspoon almond extract**
- ½ **teaspoon salt**

1. Place cherries in a food processor; cover and process until pureed. Add the remaining ingredients; cover and pulse until blended. Transfer the puree to a freezer container. Freeze 1 hour or until edges begin to firm; stir. Freeze 2 hours longer or until firm.
2. Just before serving, transfer to a blender or food processor; cover and process 2-3 minutes or until smooth.

BUTTER PECAN ICE CREAM

Is traditional butter pecan your ice cream of choice? Give this recipe a try! It's a nutty, rich indulgence I frequently take to parties. I combine the pecans with butter, salt and sugar, then pop them into the oven for 15 minutes for great toasted flavor.

—PATRICIA SIMMS DALLAS, TX

PREP: 45 MIN. + CHILLING
PROCESS: 20 MIN. + FREEZING
MAKES: ABOUT 2 QUARTS

TOASTED NUTS

- **3 tablespoons butter, melted**
- **¾ cup chopped pecans**
- **⅛ teaspoon salt**
- **1 tablespoon sugar**

ICE CREAM

- **2½ cups milk**
- **½ cup packed brown sugar**
- **¼ cup sugar**
- **2 tablespoons cornstarch**
- **2 eggs, lightly beaten**
- **1 cup heavy whipping cream**
- **⅓ cup maple-flavored pancake syrup**
- **2 teaspoons vanilla extract**

1. Preheat oven to 350°. On a baking sheet, combine the butter, pecans, salt and 1 tablespoon sugar and spread into a single layer. Roast 15 minutes. Stir and roast 15 minutes longer. Cool.

2. For ice cream, in a large saucepan, heat milk to 175°. Combine sugars and cornstarch; gradually stir into milk. Cook and stir over medium heat until thickened and bubbly. Reduce heat to low; cook and stir 2 minutes longer. Remove from heat.

3. In a small bowl, whisk a small amount of hot mixture into eggs; return all to pan, whisking constantly. Bring to a gentle boil; cook and stir 2 minutes. Remove from heat immediately.

4. Quickly transfer to a large bowl; place bowl in a pan of ice water. Stir gently and occasionally for 2 minutes. Stir in the cream, syrup and vanilla. Press plastic wrap onto the surface of the custard. Refrigerate for several hours or overnight.

5. Stir nuts into custard. Fill cylinder of ice cream freezer two-thirds full; freeze according to manufacturer's directions. (Refrigerate any remaining mixture until ready to freeze.) Transfer ice cream to freezer containers, allowing headspace for expansion. Freeze 2-4 hours or until firm. Repeat with any remaining ice cream mixture.

CREAM OF THE CROP

Heavy whipping cream ranges from 36% to 40% butterfat and doubles in volume when whipped. It is often labeled as either heavy cream or whipping cream.

CHOCOLATE MALTED ICE CREAM

As a child, I helped crank out countless gallons of homemade ice cream. Thanks to this recipe, I'm carrying on the tradition in my own family. We're huge chocolate fans—so you can imagine the reaction when I dish out bowlfuls of this!

—ROSE HARE MOUNTAIN HOME, ID

PREP: 15 MIN. + CHILLING
PROCESS: 20 MIN./BATCH + FREEZING
MAKES: 2 QUARTS

- 2 **cups milk**
- 1 **cup sugar**
- ½ **cup chocolate malted milk powder**
- 5 **eggs, lightly beaten**
- 4 **cups heavy whipping cream**
- 1 **cup malted milk balls, coarsely crushed**
- 1 **tablespoon vanilla extract**

1. In a large saucepan, heat the milk to 175°; stir in sugar and malted milk powder until dissolved. Whisk a small amount of the hot mixture into the eggs. Return to pan. Cook over low heat until mixture is just thick enough to coat a metal spoon and a thermometer reads at least 160°, stirring constantly. Do not allow to boil. Remove from the heat immediately.

2. Quickly transfer to a large bowl; place bowl in a pan of ice water. Stir gently and occasionally for 2 minutes. Stir in cream, malted milk balls and vanilla. Press plastic wrap onto surface of custard. Refrigerate several hours or overnight.

3. Fill the cylinder of ice cream freezer two-thirds full; freeze according to the manufacturer's directions. (Refrigerate remaining mixture until ready to freeze.) When ice cream is frozen, transfer to a freezer container, allowing headspace for expansion. Freeze 2-4 hours or until firm. Repeat with the remaining ice cream mixture.

FROZEN LEMON YOGURT

When I wanted a treat that would satisfy my sweet tooth without going overboard on fat and calories, I experimented until I came up with a lemony frozen yogurt.

—CAROL MEAD LOS ALAMOS, NM

PREP: 10 MIN.
FREEZE: 30 MIN. + FREEZING
MAKES: 5 CUPS

- 4 **cups (32 ounces) plain yogurt**
- 1⅔ **cups sugar**
- ⅓ **cup lemon juice**
- 1 **tablespoon grated lemon peel**
- 4 **drops yellow food coloring, optional**

1. In a bowl, combine the plain yogurt, sugar, lemon juice and lemon peel; mix well. Stir in the yellow food coloring if desired.

2. Pour mixture into cylinder of ice cream freezer; freeze according to the manufacturer's directions. Transfer ice cream to freezer containers, allowing headspace for expansion. Freeze 2-4 hours or until firm.

BLUEBERRY ICE CREAM

We're fortunate to have wild blueberries growing on our property, and they spark many ideas in the kitchen. It's no surprise that our 10 children, grandchildren and great-grandchildren prefer that we use our crop for this frosty treat.

—**ALMA MOSHER** MOHANNES, NB

PREP: 15 MIN. + CHILLING
PROCESS: 20 MIN./BATCH + FREEZING
MAKES: ABOUT 1¾ QUARTS

- **4 cups fresh or frozen blueberries**
- **2 cups sugar**
- **2 tablespoons water**
- **4 cups half-and-half cream**

1. In a large saucepan, combine berries, sugar and water. Bring to a boil. Reduce heat; simmer, uncovered, until sugar is dissolved and berries are softened. Press the mixture through a fine-mesh strainer into a bowl; discard pulp. Stir in cream. Cover and refrigerate overnight.

2. Fill cylinder of ice cream freezer two-thirds full; freeze according to the manufacturer's directions. (Refrigerate any remaining mixture until ready to freeze.) Transfer ice cream to freezer containers, allowing headspace for expansion. Freeze 2-4 hours or until firm. Repeat with any remaining ice cream mixture.

Java Crunch
Ice Cream

COFFEE FIX

Want to perk up scoops of Java Crunch Ice Cream (recipe at far right) even more for coffee lovers? Sprinkle each serving with chocolate-covered espresso beans. Look for them in your favorite specialty food store, supermarket, candy store or coffee shop.

JAVA CRUNCH ICE CREAM

My daughter just can't get enough of this chunky ice cream and begs me to make it. Instant coffee adds a wonderfully rich flavor that complements the chocolate-covered pecans and buttery toffee chips.

—JAMIE PARKER LUBBOCK, TX

PREP: 15 MIN.
PROCESS: 20 MIN./BATCH + FREEZING
MAKES: 2¾ QUARTS

- 4 **cups heavy whipping cream**
- 4 **cups half-and-half cream**
- 1 **can (14 ounces) sweetened condensed milk**
- 2 **cans (5 ounces each) evaporated milk**
- 3 **tablespoons instant coffee granules**
- 1 **teaspoon vanilla extract**
- 2 **cups pecan halves**
- 1 **cup almond brickle chips or English toffee bits**
- 8 **ounces dark chocolate candy coating, chopped**

1. In a large bowl, combine the first six ingredients. Refrigerate until chilled.

2. In a small bowl, combine the pecans and brickle chips. In a microwave, melt the dark chocolate candy coating; stir until smooth. Pour over pecan mixture. Transfer to a 15x10x1-in. pan. Refrigerate until chocolate candy coating is firm; chop and set aside.

3. Fill cylinder of ice cream freezer two-thirds full; freeze according to the manufacturer's directions. (Refrigerate the remaining mixture until ready to freeze.) Transfer ice cream to a freezer container, allowing headspace for expansion. For each batch, stir in some of the reserved pecan mixture. Freeze 2-4 hours or until firm.

FROSTY NOTES

CREAMY LIME SHERBET

PREP: 20 MIN. + FREEZING • **MAKES:** 1½ QUARTS

- 2 **cups milk**
- 1¼ **cups sugar**
- ⅓ **cup lime juice**
- 1½ **teaspoons grated lime peel**
- 2 **to 3 drops green food coloring, optional**
- 1 **carton (8 ounces) frozen whipped topping, thawed**

1. In a large saucepan, combine the milk and sugar. Cook and stir over medium heat until the sugar is dissolved and the mixture reaches 175°. Refrigerate until chilled.

2. Stir in the lime juice, lime peel and green food coloring if desired. Freeze in an ice cream freezer according to manufacturer's directions.

3. Transfer the sherbet to a 2½-qt. freezer container. Allow to soften slightly; fold in the whipped topping. Freeze for at least 4 hours before serving.

My luncheon guests are always impressed when I bring out this smooth and tangy sherbet. For an elegant finish, I garnish each serving with candied edible flowers.

—BETSY HEDEMAN TIMONIUM, MD

Creamy Lime Sherbet

Old-Time Custard
Ice Cream

OLD-TIME CUSTARD ICE CREAM

I think my most memorable summertime dessert for get-togethers has always been homemade ice cream. This traditional custard-style recipe is so rich and velvety—the perfect splurge on a hot afternoon.

—**MARTHA SELF** MONTGOMERY, TX

PREP: 55 MIN. + CHILLING
PROCESS: 55 MIN./BATCH + FREEZING
MAKES: 2¾ QUARTS

- 1½ **cups sugar**
- ¼ **cup all-purpose flour**
- ½ **teaspoon salt**
- 4 **cups whole milk**
- 4 **eggs, lightly beaten**
- 2 **pints heavy whipping cream**
- 3 **tablespoons vanilla extract**

1. In a large heavy saucepan, combine sugar, flour and salt. Gradually add milk until smooth. Cook and stir over medium heat until thickened and bubbly. Reduce heat to low; cook and stir 2 minutes longer. Remove from heat.

2. In a small bowl, whisk a small amount of hot mixture into eggs; return all to pan, whisking constantly. Bring to a gentle boil; cook and stir 2 minutes. Remove from heat immediately.

3. Quickly transfer to a large bowl; place bowl in a pan of ice water. Stir gently and occasionally for 2 minutes. Press plastic wrap onto the surface of the custard. Refrigerate for several hours or overnight.

4. Stir whipping cream and vanilla into custard. Fill cylinder of ice cream freezer two-thirds full; freeze according to manufacturer's directions. (Refrigerate the remaining mixture until ready to freeze.) Transfer the ice cream to freezer containers, allowing headspace for expansion. Freeze 2-4 hours or until firm. Repeat with the remaining ice cream mixture.

FROSTY NOTES

CHERRY NUT ICE CREAM

Loaded with almonds, coconut, chocolate and cherries, this is a family favorite.

—MARY LOU PATRICK EAST WENATCHEE, WA

PREP: 30 MIN. + CHILLING
PROCESS: 20 MIN./BATCH + FREEZING
MAKES: 1½ QUARTS

- 6 **cups heavy whipping cream**
- 1 **cup sugar**
- ⅛ **teaspoon salt**
- 3 **egg yolks**
- 3 **teaspoons almond extract**
- 2 **cups fresh or frozen pitted dark sweet cherries, thawed and cut into quarters**
- 1 **cup flaked coconut, toasted**
- 1 **cup sliced almonds, toasted**
- 1 **milk chocolate candy bar (7 ounces), chopped**

1. In a saucepan, heat cream over medium heat until bubbles form around sides of saucepan; stir in sugar and salt until dissolved. Whisk a small amount of the cream into the egg yolks. Return all to pan, whisking constantly. Cook over low heat until the mixture is just thick enough to coat a metal spoon and a thermometer reads at least 160°, stirring constantly. Do not allow to boil. Remove from heat immediately.

2. Cool quickly by placing bowl in a pan of ice water. Stir gently and occasionally for 2 minutes. Stir in almond extract. Press plastic wrap onto the surface of the custard. Refrigerate for several hours or overnight.

3. Fill cylinder of ice cream freezer two-thirds full; freeze according to the manufacturer's directions. (Refrigerate any remaining mixture until ready to freeze.) In each batch, stir cherries, coconut, almonds and chocolate into ice cream just until combined. Transfer the ice cream to freezer containers, allowing headspace for expansion. Freeze 2-4 hours or until firm.

RHUBARB ICE CREAM

After tasting rhubarb ice cream, I wanted to make my own using my homegrown stalks.

—DENISE LINNETT PICTON, ON

PREP: 45 MIN. + CHILLING
PROCESS: 20 MIN. + FREEZING
MAKES: 1 QUART

- 3 **cups sliced fresh or frozen rhubarb**
- 2 **cups sugar**
- 1 **cup milk**
- 1 **cup heavy whipping cream**
- 2 **teaspoons lemon juice**
- 1 **teaspoon minced fresh gingerroot**

1. Preheat oven to 375°. Place rhubarb in an ungreased 13x9x2-in. baking dish. Sprinkle with sugar; toss to coat. Cover and bake 30-40 minutes or until tender, stirring occasionally.

2. Cool slightly. Process the rhubarb in batches in a food processor; transfer to a bowl. Cover; refrigerate until chilled.

3. In a large bowl, combine milk, cream, lemon juice and ginger; stir in rhubarb.

4. Fill cylinder of ice cream freezer two-thirds full; freeze according to the manufacturer's directions. (Refrigerate any remaining mixture until ready to freeze.) Transfer ice cream to freezer containers, allowing headspace for expansion. Freeze 2-4 hours or until firm. Repeat with any remaining ice cream mixture.

ZESTY LEMON GRANITA

Here's a light dessert with a refreshing icy texture. One person dubbed it "the most lemony thing I've ever eaten."

—SONYA LABBE WEST HOLLYWOOD, CA

PREP: 15 MIN. + FREEZING
MAKES: 2 CUPS

- 1 **cup water**
- ⅔ **cup sugar**
- ⅔ **cup lemon juice**
- 2 **fresh thyme sprigs**
- 2 **teaspoons grated lemon peel**

1. In a small saucepan, bring the water and sugar to a boil. Cook and stir until the sugar is dissolved. Remove from the heat; stir in the lemon juice and thyme. Transfer to an 8-in.-square dish; cool to room temperature.

2. Remove thyme. Freeze for 1 hour; stir with a fork. Freeze 2-3 hours longer or until completely frozen, stirring every 30 minutes.

3. Stir the granita with a fork just before serving; spoon into dessert dishes. Garnish with lemon peel.

COFFEE ICE CREAM

I combined two yummy recipes—one for a special coffee sauce and the other for vanilla ice cream—to create this treat. I serve it plain in bowls so the mild coffee flavor really comes through.

—THERESA HANSEN PENSACOLA, FL

PREP: 30 MIN. + FREEZING
MAKES: 1½ QUARTS

- ¼ **cup sugar**
- 1 **tablespoon cornstarch**
- 1 **tablespoon instant coffee granules**
- 2 **tablespoons butter, melted**
- 1 **cup milk**
- 1 **teaspoon vanilla extract**
- 1 **can (14 ounces) sweetened condensed milk**
- 2 **cups heavy whipping cream**

1. In a large saucepan, combine the sugar, cornstarch, coffee and butter until blended. Stir in the milk. Bring to a boil over medium heat; cook and stir for 2 minutes or until thickened. Remove from heat; stir in vanilla. Cool completely. Stir in condensed milk.

2. In a large bowl, beat the cream until stiff peaks form; fold into milk mixture. Pour into a 9-in. pan. Cover and freeze 6 hours or until firm.

GREAT GRANITA

Granitas don't require an ice cream freezer. The sugary flavored mixture needs to be stirred often as it freezes to produce its characteristic crystalline texture.

MAPLE-WALNUT ICE CREAM

When my family is planning a get-together, I usually receive a request to bring along my nutty maple-flavored ice cream.

—SANDY MCKENZIE BRAHAM, MN

PREP: 20 MIN. + CHILLING
PROCESS: 20 MIN. + FREEZING
MAKES: 1 QUART

- 1 **cup whole milk**
- 2 **eggs, lightly beaten**
- ½ **cup honey**
- 2 **cups heavy whipping cream**
- 1½ **teaspoons maple flavoring**
- ½ **cup chopped walnuts, toasted**

1. In a small saucepan, heat the milk to 175°. Combine eggs and honey. Whisk a small amount of the hot mixture into the egg mixture. Return all to the pan, whisking constantly.

2. Cook over low heat until mixture coats the back of a metal spoon and a thermometer reads at least 160°, stirring constantly. Do not allow to boil. Remove from heat immediately.

3. Quickly transfer to a large bowl; place bowl in a pan of ice water. Stir gently and occasionally for 2 minutes. Stir in the heavy whipping cream and maple flavoring. Press plastic wrap onto surface of custard. Refrigerate several hours or overnight.

4. Fill cylinder of ice cream freezer two-thirds full; freeze according to the manufacturer's directions. For each batch, add some of the nuts during the 5 minutes of processing. (Refrigerate any remaining mixture until ready to freeze.) Transfer the ice cream to freezer containers, allowing headspace for expansion. Freeze 2-4 hours or until firm.

GRAPE SHERBET

My husband, daughters and I first enjoyed this pretty lavender sherbet at our friends' house. They graciously shared the recipe after we all raved about it. Now I make it for parties and other events.

—SHERRY ROMINGER ROGERS, AR

PREP: 5 MIN.
PROCESS: 20 MIN. + FREEZING
MAKES: 1 QUART

- 1¾ **cups grape juice**
- 3 **tablespoons lemon juice**
- ½ **cup sugar**
- 1¾ **cups half-and-half cream**

In a large bowl, combine all the ingredients. Fill the cylinder of ice cream freezer two-thirds full; freeze according to the manufacturer's directions. Transfer sherbet to freezer container, allowing headspace for expansion. Freeze 4 hours or until firm.

BUTTERFINGER ICE CREAM

With crushed Butterfinger candy bars, this from-the-freezer treat never lasts long.

—TAMMY DROST CHEYENNE, WY

PREP: 10 MIN.
PROCESS: 20 MIN./BATCH + FREEZING
MAKES: 4 QUARTS

- ½ **gallon whole milk**
- 1 **can (14 ounces) sweetened condensed milk**
- 1 **carton (16 ounces) frozen whipped topping, thawed**
- 6 **Butterfinger candy bars (2.1 ounces each), crushed**

1. In a large bowl, whisk milk and condensed milk. Whisk in whipped topping until combined; stir in the crushed candy bars.

2. Fill cylinder of ice cream freezer two-thirds full; freeze according to the manufacturer's directions. (Refrigerate the remaining mixture until ready to freeze.) Transfer ice cream to freezer containers, allowing headspace for expansion. Freeze 2-4 hours or until firm. Repeat with the remaining ice cream mixture.

CLOSED CONE

Love ice cream in a crunchy sugar cone or waffle cone? The hole in the bottom of these cones can make for messy hands. To avoid dripping ice cream, tuck a miniature marshmallow or two into the bottom of the cone before you scoop in the ice cream.

LIGHTENED UP LEMON CUSTARD ICE CREAM

Indulge without the guilt! I think this light ice cream matches the wonderful yet heavier original in taste and texture.

—LINDA TIPTON ROANOKE RAPIDS, NC

PREP: 15 MIN. + CHILLING
PROCESSING: 20 MIN./BATCH + FREEZING
MAKES: 2 QUARTS

- 1¾ **cups sugar**
- ⅓ **cup all-purpose flour**
- ¼ **teaspoon salt**
- 3 **cups milk**
- 2 **eggs, lightly beaten**
- 2 **tablespoons apple jelly**
- 3 **cups fat-free half-and-half**
- 1 **cup (8 ounces) fat-free sour cream**
- 1 **cup lemon juice**

1. In a large saucepan, combine the sugar, flour and salt. Gradually add the milk. Cook and stir over medium heat until thickened and bubbly. Reduce heat to low; cook and stir 2 minutes longer. Remove from heat.

2. In a small bowl, whisk a small amount of hot mixture into eggs; return all to pan, whisking constantly. Bring to a gentle boil; cook and stir 2 minutes. Remove from the heat immediately; stir in jelly until melted.

3. Quickly transfer to a large bowl; place bowl in a pan of ice water. Stir gently and occasionally for 2 minutes. Stir in half-and-half, sour cream and lemon juice. Press plastic wrap onto surface of custard. Refrigerate several hours or overnight.

4. Fill cylinder of ice cream freezer two-thirds full; freeze according to the manufacturer's directions. (Refrigerate the remaining mixture until ready to freeze.) Transfer ice cream to freezer containers, allowing headspace for expansion. Freeze 2-4 hours or until firm. Repeat with the remaining ice cream mixture.

LAVENDER ICE CREAM

Herbal ice cream is always a favorite at our house. A scoop of lavender is heavenly on warm peach crisp or blueberry cobbler!

—SUE GRONHOLZ BEAVER DAM, WI

PREP: 15 MIN. + CHILLING
PROCESS: 20 MIN. + FREEZING
MAKES: 1 PINT

- ⅔ **cup half-and-half cream**
- ⅓ **cup fresh lavender flowers or 2 tablespoons dried lavender flowers**
- ⅔ **cup sugar**
- 4 **egg yolks, beaten**
- ⅔ **cup heavy whipping cream**

1. In a small saucepan, heat half-and-half to 175°. Remove from heat; add lavender. Cover and steep 20 minutes. Strain, discarding lavender.

2. Return half-and-half to the heat; stir in sugar until dissolved. Whisk a small amount of the hot mixture into egg yolks; return all to pan, whisking constantly. Cook and stir over low heat until mixture reaches at least 160° and coats the back of a spoon.

3. Cool quickly by placing pan in a bowl of ice water; stir for 2 minutes. Stir in whipping cream. Press waxed paper onto surface of custard. Chill several hours or overnight.

4. Fill cylinder of ice cream freezer two-thirds full; freeze according to the manufacturer's directions. Transfer ice cream to a freezer container; freeze for 2-4 hours before serving.

NOTE: *Look for dried lavender flowers in spice shops. If using lavender from the garden, make sure it hasn't been treated with chemicals.*

SUPER STRAWBERRY SHERBET

This cool, smooth summertime treat is nice to have ready in the freezer when family members or friends drop by.

—ANNE DICKENS SARASOTA, FL

PREP: 10 MIN. + STANDING
PROCESS: 20 MIN. + FREEZING
MAKES: ABOUT 1 GALLON

- 4 **quarts fresh strawberries, sliced**
- 4 **cups sugar**
- 2⅔ **cups milk**
- ⅔ **cup orange juice**
- ⅛ **teaspoon ground cinnamon**

1. In a large bowl, combine strawberries and sugar; let stand until juicy, about 1½ hours. Process in batches in a blender until pureed. Add milk, orange juice and cinnamon; cover and process until blended.

2. Fill cylinder of ice cream freezer two-thirds full; freeze according to manufacturer's directions. Refrigerate remaining mixture until ready to freeze. Transfer sherbet to freezer containers, allowing headspace for expansion. Freeze 2-4 hours or until firm. Repeat with remaining sherbet mixture.

LEMON 'N' LIME STRAWBERRY ICE

Surprise guests with this icy dessert after dinner on a warm summer evening.

—MARIE RIZZIO INTERLOCHEN, MI

PREP: 30 MIN. + FREEZING
MAKES: 6 SERVINGS

- 1 **cup sugar**
- ¾ **cup water**
- 1 **tablespoon shredded orange peel**
- 2 **teaspoons shredded lemon peel**
- 1½ **teaspoons shredded lime peel**
- ⅓ **cup orange juice**
- 3 **tablespoons lemon juice**
- 2 **tablespoons lime juice**
- 4 **cups sliced fresh strawberries**

1. In a small saucepan, combine the first five ingredients. Bring to a boil. Reduce the heat; simmer, uncovered, 5-6 minutes or until slightly thickened. Strain; discard peels. Add juices to the syrup; cool slightly.

2. Place half of the juice mixture and strawberries in a blender; cover and pulse until nearly smooth. Pour into a 2-qt. freezer container. Repeat with remaining juice mixture and berries.

3. Cover; freeze 12 hours or overnight, stirring several times. Ice may be frozen for up to 3 months. Just before serving, break apart with a large spoon.

BERRY GOOD

When choosing fresh strawberries, look for brightly colored, plump, fragrant berries with the green hulls intact. Avoid any berries that are soft, shriveled or moldy. Wash them before removing the hulls. One pint of berries yields 1½ to 2 cups sliced.

Lemon 'n' Lime
Strawberry Ice

PEACH GELATO

This lovely Italian gelato filled with fresh peaches and spiked with schnapps tastes as good as it looks. If you'd rather not have the liqueur, simply leave it out.

—MOLLY HAEN BALDWIN, WI

PREP: 25 MIN. + CHILLING
PROCESS: 20 MIN. + FREEZING • **MAKES:** 1 QUART

- 3 **cups sliced peeled peaches**
- 2 **tablespoons water**
- 2 **cups whole milk**
- ¾ **cup sugar**
- 4 **egg yolks, beaten**
- 1 **cup heavy whipping cream**
- 1 **tablespoon peach schnapps liqueur, optional**

1. Place peaches and water in a large skillet; cook, uncovered, over medium heat until tender. Place in a food processor; cover and process until blended. Set aside.
2. In a small saucepan, heat milk to 175°; stir in sugar until dissolved. Whisk a small amount of the hot mixture into egg yolks. Return all to the pan, whisking constantly. Cook over low heat until mixture is just thick enough to coat a metal spoon and a thermometer reads at least 160°, stirring constantly. Do not allow to boil. Remove from heat immediately.
3. Quickly transfer to a large bowl; place bowl in a pan of ice water. Stir gently and occasionally for 2 minutes. Stir in the heavy whipping cream, peaches and liqueur if desired. Press plastic wrap onto surface of custard. Refrigerate several hours or overnight.
4. Fill cylinder of ice cream freezer two-thirds full; freeze according to the manufacturer's directions. (Refrigerate any remaining mixture until ready to freeze.) Transfer ice cream to freezer containers, allowing headspace for expansion. Freeze 2-4 hours or until firm. Repeat with any remaining gelato mixture.

Peach Gelato

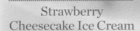

Strawberry
Cheesecake Ice Cream

PEEL APPEAL

The peel from citrus fruit adds a burst of flavor to recipes and color to garnishes. Citrus peel, also called zest, can be grated into fine shreds with a Microplane grater. Remove only the colored portion of the peel, not the bitter white pith.

STRAWBERRY CHEESECAKE ICE CREAM

PREP: 10 MIN. + FREEZING
MAKES: 2 QUARTS

- 1 **package (8 ounces) cream cheese, softened**
- ⅓ **cup refrigerated French vanilla nondairy creamer**
- ¼ **cup sugar**
- 1 **teaspoon grated lemon peel**
- 1 **carton (16 ounces) frozen whipped topping, thawed**
- 2 **packages (10 ounces each) frozen sweetened sliced strawberries, thawed**

In a large bowl, beat the cream cheese, creamer, sugar and lemon peel until blended. Fold in the whipped topping and strawberries. Transfer to a freezer container; freeze for 4 hours or until firm. Remove from freezer 10 minutes before serving.

Cheesecake-flavored ice cream? Yes, please! This dreamy creation is great whether served in a bowl or scooped into cones. Plus, I've found it doesn't melt as fast as regular ice cream.
—DEBRA GOFORTH NEWPORT, TN

PEACH ICE CREAM

I didn't think my mother-in-law's incredible vanilla ice cream could get any better—until I stirred in chopped peaches! My boys think it's the greatest and say it tastes best served outdoors under a shady tree.
—LISA TENBARGE HAUBSTADT, IN

PREP: 30 MIN. + CHILLING
PROCESS: 20 MIN. + FREEZING
MAKES: 1¼ QUARTS

- 1 **cup sugar**
- 1 **cup milk**
- 1 **egg, beaten**
- 3⅓ **cups heavy whipping cream**
- ¼ **cup instant vanilla pudding mix**
- 1½ **cups finely chopped fresh or frozen peaches, thawed**
- 2 **teaspoons vanilla extract**

1. In a large saucepan, combine sugar, milk and egg. Cook over low heat until mixture is just thick enough to coat a metal spoon and a thermometer reads at least 160°, stirring constantly. Do not allow to boil. Remove from heat immediately.

2. Quickly transfer to a large bowl; place bowl in a pan of ice water. Stir gently and occasionally for 2 minutes. Press plastic wrap onto the surface of the custard. Refrigerate several hours or overnight.

3. Stir cream, pudding mix, peaches and vanilla into custard. Fill cylinder of an ice cream freezer two-thirds full. Freeze according to manufacturer's directions. (Refrigerate any remaining mixture until ready to freeze.) Transfer the ice cream to freezer containers, allowing headspace for expansion. Freeze 2-4 hours or until firm. Repeat with any remaining ice cream mixture.

FRESH MINT & GRAPEFRUIT SORBET

The mint really balances the tartness of the ruby red grapefruit juice in my sorbet.
—LISA SPEER PALM BEACH, FL

PREP: 20 MIN. + FREEZING
MAKES: 1½ QUARTS

- 2 **cups sugar**
- 2 **cups water**
- 1 **cup fresh mint leaves**
- 4 **cups ruby red grapefruit juice**

1. In a small saucepan, bring the sugar, water and mint to a boil. Reduce heat to low; cook for 5 minutes. Remove from heat; let stand 10 minutes. Strain and discard mint leaves. Stir in grapefruit juice. Allow mixture to cool completely.

2. Fill the cylinder of ice cream freezer two-thirds full; freeze according to the manufacturer's directions. (Refrigerate the remaining mixture until ready to freeze.) Transfer sorbet to a freezer container, allowing headspace for expansion. Freeze 4 hours or until firm. Repeat with remaining sorbet mixture.

APPLE STREUSEL ICE CREAM

Anyone who likes traditional apple pie will love this frosty take on the classic dessert. Every spoonful bursts with bits of sauteed fruit, rich caramel topping, cinnamon and a sensational homemade streusel mixture. You'll definitely want more than one scoop!

—KAREN DELGADO SHAWNEE, KS

PREP: 35 MIN. + CHILLING
PROCESS: 20 MIN. + FREEZING
MAKES: 1½ QUARTS

- ⅓ **cup packed brown sugar**
- ¼ **cup all-purpose flour**
- ½ **teaspoon ground cinnamon**
- 3 **tablespoons plus 4½ teaspoons cold butter, divided**
- ½ **cup chopped pecans**
- 1 **cup chopped peeled Golden Delicious apple**
- 2 **teaspoons sugar**
- ¼ **teaspoon ground cinnamon**

ICE CREAM
- 1¼ **cups milk**
- ¾ **cup sugar**
- 1¾ **cups heavy whipping cream**
- 1½ **teaspoons vanilla extract**
- 1 **jar (12 ounces) caramel ice cream topping**

1. Preheat oven to 350°. For streusel, combine the brown sugar, flour and cinnamon in a bowl; cut in 3 tablespoons butter until mixture resembles coarse crumbs. Stir in pecans.

2. Press into a 9-in. pie plate. Bake 10-12 minutes or until the edges are browned. Cool slightly; break into small pieces. Cool completely.

3. In a small skillet, melt remaining butter. Stir in the apple, sugar and cinnamon. Cook 8-10 minutes or until the apple is tender; cool.

4. In a large saucepan, heat the milk to 175°; stir in the sugar until dissolved. Cool. In a large bowl, combine the milk mixture, cream and vanilla. Refrigerate for several hours or overnight.

5. Fill the cylinder of ice cream freezer two-thirds full; freeze according to the manufacturer's directions, adding apple mixture during the last 5 minutes of processing.

6. Spoon a third of the ice cream into a freezer container. Top with a third of the streusel mixture. Drizzle with a third of the caramel topping. Repeat layers once. Top with the remaining ice cream. With a spatula, cut through the ice cream in several places to gently swirl layers. Cover; freeze overnight. Garnish with the remaining streusel and caramel topping.

Lemon Gelato

While on vacation in Italy, I became obsessed with gelato. My favorite choice was lemon because the Italian fruit has such an intense flavor.

—**GAIL WANG** TROY, MI

LEMON GELATO

PREP: 30 MIN. • **PROCESS:** 20 MIN. + FREEZING
MAKES: 1½ QUARTS

1   **cup milk**
1   **cup sugar**
5   **egg yolks, lightly beaten**
3   **tablespoons grated lemon peel**
¾   **cup lemon juice**
2   **cups heavy whipping cream**

1. In a small heavy saucepan, heat the milk to 175°; stir in sugar until dissolved. Whisk a small amount of hot mixture into yolks. Return all to the pan, whisking constantly. Add peel. Cook over low heat until mixture is just thick enough to coat a metal spoon and a thermometer reads at least 160°, stirring constantly. Do not allow to boil. Remove from heat immediately. Stir in juice.

2. Quickly transfer to a large bowl; place bowl in a pan of ice water. Stir gently and occasionally for 2 minutes. Stir in cream. Press plastic wrap onto the surface of the custard. Refrigerate several hours or overnight.

3. Fill cylinder of ice cream freezer two-thirds full; freeze according to the manufacturer's directions. (Refrigerate remaining mixture until ready to freeze.) Transfer ice cream to freezer containers, allowing headspace for expansion. Freeze 2-4 hours or until firm. Repeat with remaining ice cream mixture.

FROSTY NOTES

FROSTY
DESSERTS

STRAWBERRY SORBET SENSATION

PREP: 20 MIN. + FREEZING • **MAKES:** 8 SERVINGS

- 2 **cups strawberry sorbet, softened if necessary**
- 1 **cup cold fat-free milk**
- 1 **package (1 ounce) sugar-free instant vanilla pudding mix**
- 1 **carton (8 ounces) frozen reduced-fat whipped topping, thawed**
  Sliced fresh strawberries

1. Line an 8x4-in. loaf pan with foil. Spread sorbet onto bottom of pan; place in freezer 15 minutes.

2. In a small bowl, whisk milk and pudding mix 2 minutes. Let stand 2 minutes or until soft-set. Fold whipped topping into pudding; spread over sorbet. Freeze the dessert, covered, 4 hours or overnight.

3. Remove from freezer 10-15 minutes before serving. Unmold dessert onto a serving plate; remove foil. Cut dessert into slices. Serve with fresh strawberries.

On hot days in Colorado, we chill out with slices of this berries-and-cream dessert. The layered effect is so much fun. Use any flavor of sorbet you like.
—**KENDRA DOSS** COLORADO SPRINGS, CO

COCONUT-PINEAPPLE SHERBET TORTE

I made up this torte one afternoon and when I served it that night, it vanished within minutes. That's when I knew I'd struck gold.

—JONI HILTON ROCKLIN, CA

PREP: 25 MIN. + FREEZING
MAKES: 10 SERVINGS

- 1 **package (10 to 12 ounces) white baking chips**
- 1 **cup flaked coconut**
- 1 **cup cream of coconut**
- 2 **cups crushed crisp oatmeal cookies (about 20)**
- ⅓ **cup butter, melted**
- 4 **cups pineapple or other tropical-flavored sherbet, slightly softened if necessary**

1. In a small saucepan, combine baking chips, coconut and cream of coconut; cook and stir over medium heat until chips are melted. Cool completely.

2. Line a 9x5-in. loaf pan with plastic wrap, letting edges extend over sides. In a small bowl, mix crushed cookies and butter.

3. To assemble, spoon 2 cups sherbet into prepared pan, spreading evenly. Sprinkle with half of the cookie mixture; press to make a firm layer. Spread with half of the coconut mixture. Repeat layers. Wrap the torte securely and freeze overnight.

4. Lifting with plastic wrap, unmold the torte onto a serving plate. Cut torte lengthwise in half; cut each half crosswise into slices. Serve immediately.

CARAMEL TOFFEE ICE CREAM PIE

This delicious, decadent pie is a snap to make. Fat-free frozen yogurt has never tasted so good.

—DIANE LOMBARDO NEW CASTLE, PA

PREP: 25 MIN. + FREEZING
MAKES: 8 SERVINGS

- 1½ **cups chocolate graham cracker crumbs (about 8 whole crackers)**
- 2 **tablespoons sugar**
- 1 **egg white, beaten**
- 2 **tablespoons butter, melted**
- 4 **cups fat-free vanilla frozen yogurt, softened, divided**
- 2 **English toffee candy bars (1.4 ounces each), coarsely chopped, divided**
- ½ **cup caramel ice cream topping, divided**

1. Preheat oven to 375°. In a small bowl, combine cracker crumbs and sugar; stir in egg white and butter. Press onto the bottom and up the sides of a 9-in. pie plate coated with cooking spray. Bake 6-8 minutes or until set. Cool completely on a wire rack.

2. Spread 2⅔ cups of frozen yogurt into the crust. Sprinkle with half of the toffee bits; drizzle with half of caramel. Layer with remaining yogurt, toffee and caramel topping.

3. Cover and freeze for 8 hours or overnight. Remove from the freezer 15 minutes before serving.

BLACK FOREST FREEZER PIE

Keep this cool take on a delightful German classic tucked away in the freezer. I sometimes make it with strawberry pie filling and a chocolate crust.

—ANGIE HELMS PONTOTOC, MS

PREP: 20 MIN. + FREEZING
MAKES: 6-8 SERVINGS

- 1 **pint chocolate or vanilla ice cream, softened**
- 1 **extra-servings-size graham cracker crust (9 ounces)**
- 4 **ounces cream cheese, softened**
- 1 **cup confectioners' sugar**
- 1 **carton (8 ounces) frozen whipped topping, thawed**
- 1 **can (21 ounces) cherry pie filling, chilled**
- 3 **tablespoons chocolate syrup**

1. Spoon ice cream into pie crust; cover and freeze 15 minutes.

2. Meanwhile, in a large bowl, beat cream cheese and confectioners' sugar until smooth; fold in whipped topping. Set aside 1½ cups for garnish.

3. Spread remaining cream cheese mixture over ice cream. Using the back of a spoon, make an 8-in.-diameter well in the center of the pie for pie filling (do not add filling). Pipe reserved cream cheese mixture around pie.

4. Cover and freeze 3-4 hours or until firm. May be frozen up to 2 months. Just before serving, spoon pie filling into the well; drizzle with chocolate syrup. Serve immediately.

FROZEN MACAROON DESSERT

Enjoy a sweet slice of frozen summertime bliss. With all the flavors of paradise, this irresistible treat will whisk you away to a tropical staycation.

—MAVIS GANNELLO OAK PARK, IL

PREP: 25 MIN. + FREEZING
MAKES: 12 SERVINGS

- **3 cups crumbled soft macaroon cookies**
- **1 can (20 ounces) crushed pineapple**
- **½ gallon butter pecan ice cream, softened**
- **½ cup chopped macadamia nuts**
- **1 carton (8 ounces) frozen whipped topping, thawed**

1. Preheat oven to 350°. Sprinkle cookie crumbs onto an ungreased baking sheet. Bake 8-10 minutes or until golden brown. Cool completely. Increase oven temperature to 400°.
2. Drain pineapple, reserving ¼ cup juice; set pineapple aside. In a small bowl, combine cookie crumbs and reserved juice until crumbly; set aside and refrigerate 3 tablespoons for topping.
3. Press remaining crumb mixture onto the bottom and 1 in. up the sides of an ungreased 9-in. springform pan. Bake 8-10 minutes or until lightly browned. Cool 10 minutes.
4. In a large bowl, combine ice cream, pineapple and nuts; spread over crust. Cover and freeze until firm.
5. Carefully run a knife around edge of pan to loosen. Remove sides of pan. Spread whipped topping over top. Sprinkle with reserved crumb mixture. Let dessert stand at room temperature 15 minutes before serving.

CHOCOLATE WAFER ICE CREAM

Orange and chocolate create a delicious combo in this effortless dessert. Chocolate wafers make an easy garnish.

—LILY JULOW LAWRENCEVILLE, GA

PREP: 5 MIN. + FREEZING
MAKES: 2 SERVINGS

- **8 chocolate wafers, divided**
- **1½ cups vanilla ice cream, softened**
- **2 tablespoons orange marmalade**

1. Crush two chocolate wafers. In a small bowl, beat ice cream and marmalade until blended. Fold in crushed wafers. Freeze until firm.
2. Divide ice cream between two dessert dishes. Serve with remaining chocolate wafers.

FROZEN TIRAMISU

Java fans will jump for this frosty mocha dessert. Because it requires time to freeze, it's a great make-ahead option for holidays and dinner parties.

—APRIL HARMON GREENEVILLE, TN

PREP: 20 MIN. + FREEZING
MAKES: 12 SERVINGS

- ¼ cup strong brewed coffee
- 4 teaspoons rum
- 1 package (3 ounces) soft ladyfingers, split
- 2 quarts coffee ice cream, softened
- 2 ounces bittersweet chocolate, grated
- 1 carton (8 ounces) mascarpone cheese
- 3 tablespoons coffee liqueur
- 1 tablespoon sugar
- ⅓ cup half-and-half cream
  Additional bittersweet chocolate, grated

1. Line a 9x5-in. loaf pan with plastic wrap, letting edges hang over sides; set aside. In a small bowl, combine coffee and rum; brush over the ladyfingers. Arrange ladyfingers over bottom and around sides of prepared pan, rounded sides out.

2. In a large bowl, combine ice cream and chocolate; spread into pan. Freeze overnight or until firm.

3. For sauce, in a small bowl, combine cheese, liqueur and sugar. Stir in cream until smooth.

4. To serve, unmold dessert, using ends of plastic wrap to lift from pan. Remove plastic. Cut into slices. Serve with mascarpone sauce and garnish with additional grated chocolate.

Frozen Tiramisu

SWIRLED SHERBET DESSERT

Lemon and orange sherbets are swirled over a coconut-pecan cookie crust in this refreshing dessert. It will put you in a tropical state of mind.

—AGNES WARD STRATFORD, ON

PREP: 25 MIN. + FREEZING
MAKES: 12 SERVINGS

- 1 **cup crushed vanilla wafers (about 30 wafers)**
- ⅓ **cup flaked coconut**
- ⅓ **cup chopped pecans**
- ¼ **cup butter, melted**
- 1 **pint lemon sherbet, softened**
- 1 **pint orange sherbet, softened**

1. Preheat oven to 350°. In a small bowl, combine wafer crumbs, coconut, pecans and butter; press onto the bottom of an ungreased 9-in. springform pan. Bake 10-12 minutes or until lightly browned. Cool 10 minutes on a wire rack.

2. Arrange scoops of sherbet over crust, alternating flavors. Cut through sherbet with a knife to swirl. Cover and freeze overnight. Remove from the freezer 15 minutes before serving.

LEMON MERINGUE ICE CREAM PIE

This stunning pie has it all—a nutty graham cracker crust that's layered with vanilla ice cream, tart lemon curd and beautifully browned meringue.

—DANA HINCK PENSACOLA, FL

PREP: 50 MIN. + FREEZING
MAKES: 8 SERVINGS

- 1 **cup graham cracker crumbs**
- ¾ **cup finely chopped pecans**
- ¼ **cup sugar**
- ¼ **cup butter, melted**

FILLING

- 1 **quart vanilla ice cream, softened, divided**
- 1 **jar (10 ounces) lemon curd**
- 2 **tablespoons lemon juice**

MERINGUE

- 4 **egg whites**
- 6 **tablespoons sugar**
- ¼ **teaspoon cream of tartar**

1. Combine cracker crumbs, pecans, sugar and butter; press onto bottom and up sides of an ungreased 9-in. pie plate. Bake at 400° for 10-12 minutes or until lightly browned. Cool on a wire rack. Freeze 30 minutes.

2. Spread 2 cups ice cream into crust. Freeze 30 minutes. In a small bowl, combine lemon curd and lemon juice. Spread over ice cream and freeze until firm, about 1 hour. Top with remaining ice cream. Freeze 2 hours or until set.

3. In a large heavy saucepan, combine egg whites, sugar and cream of tartar. With a hand mixer, beat on low speed 1 minute. Continue beating over low heat until mixture reaches 160°, about 8 minutes. Transfer to a large bowl; beat until stiff glossy peaks form and sugar is dissolved.

4. Immediately spread meringue over ice cream, sealing to edges of pie. Heat with a kitchen torch or broil 8 in. from the heat 3-5 minutes or until meringue is lightly browned. Freeze at least 1 hour before serving.

S'MORE ICE CREAM PIE

Our pretty s'more pie will make you glad you're not camping! Boys and girls will adore the hot toasty marshmallows atop rocky road ice cream.
—*TASTE OF HOME* **TEST KITCHEN**

PREP: 20 MIN. + FREEZING
MAKES: 4 SERVINGS

- ⅔ **cup graham cracker crumbs**
- 2 **tablespoons sugar**
- 3 **tablespoons butter, melted**
- 2½ **cups rocky road ice cream, softened**
- ⅔ **cup marshmallow creme**
- ¾ **cup miniature marshmallows**

1. Preheat oven to 325°. In a small bowl, combine cracker crumbs and sugar; stir in butter. Press onto the bottom and up the sides of a 7-in. pie plate coated with cooking spray. Bake 7-9 minutes or until lightly browned. Cool on a wire rack.
2. Spread ice cream into crust; freeze until firm. Spread the marshmallow creme over ice cream. Top with the marshmallows; gently press into creme. Cover and freeze 4 hours or overnight.
3. Just before serving, broil 6 in. from the heat for 1-2 minutes or until marshmallows are golden brown.

FROZEN LIME CAKE

This is just the thing for block parties, cookouts or any time you need a supercool dessert. The crust is a snap, and the ice cream and sherbet layers are delicious. Everyone loves it!
—**KATHY GILLOGLY** SUN CITY, CA

PREP: 15 MIN. + FREEZING
MAKES: 9 SERVINGS

- 1½ **cups ground almonds**
- ¾ **cup crushed gingersnap cookies (about 15 cookies)**
- ⅓ **cup butter, melted**
- 2 **pints pineapple-coconut or vanilla ice cream, softened**
- 2 **pints lime sherbet, softened**
  Whipped topping, optional

1. In a small bowl, combine almonds, cookies and butter. Press onto the bottom of a 9-in.-square pan. Freeze 15 minutes.
2. Spread ice cream over crust. Cover and freeze at least 30 minutes. Top with sherbet. Cover and freeze 4 hours or overnight.
3. Remove from the freezer 10 minutes before serving. Garnish servings with whipped topping if desired.

S'MORE SUNDAE

For a quick frozen s'more treat, top ice cream with fudge sauce, mini marshmallows, whipped cream and Teddy Grahams or graham cracker crumbs.

BUTTER BRICKLE ICE CREAM PIE

This is my husband's absolute favorite summertime dessert. I often serve it to company in warm-weather months. Everyone loves the rich, buttery flavor and bits of toffee crunch.

—BRENDA JACKSON GARDEN CITY, KS

PREP: 20 MIN. + FREEZING
MAKES: 8 SERVINGS

- ½ **gallon vanilla ice cream, softened,**
- 1 **graham cracker crust (9 inches)**
- ½ **cup English toffee bits or almond brickle chips**

SAUCE
- 1 **cup sugar**
- 1 **can (5 ounces) evaporated milk, divided**
- ¼ **cup dark corn syrup**
- ¼ **cup butter, cubed**
- ⅛ **teaspoon salt**
- 1 **tablespoon cornstarch**
- ½ **cup English toffee bits or almond brickle chips**

1. Spread half of the ice cream into crust. Sprinkle with toffee bits. Spoon remaining ice cream over top. Cover and freeze until firm.

2. In a large saucepan, combine the sugar, 3 tablespoons milk, corn syrup, butter and salt. Bring to a boil over medium heat. Combine cornstarch and remaining milk until smooth; gradually add to sugar mixture.

3. Return to a boil, stirring constantly. Cook and stir for 1-2 minutes or until thickened. Cool to room temperature, stirring several times. Stir in toffee bits. Refrigerate until serving.

4. Just before serving, transfer sauce to a small microwave-safe bowl. Microwave, uncovered, on high for 30-60 seconds or until heated through, stirring once. Serve with pie.

Peanut Butter
Cup Napoleons

PEANUT BUTTER CUP NAPOLEONS

PREP: 10 MIN. • **BAKE:** 15 MIN. + COOLING
MAKES: 4 SERVINGS

1   **sheet frozen puff pastry, thawed**
2   **cups peanut butter ice cream with peanut butter cup pieces, softened**
¾   **cup butterscotch-caramel ice cream topping**
3   **tablespoons creamy peanut butter**
¼   **cup chopped chocolate-covered peanuts**

1. Preheat oven to 400°. Unfold puff pastry. Cut into eight 4½x2¼-in. rectangles. Place on a greased baking sheet. Bake 12-15 minutes or until golden brown. Cool completely on a wire rack.
2. Scoop ½ cup ice cream onto each of four pastries. Top with remaining pastries. Freeze until serving.
3. Combine ice cream topping and peanut butter in a small microwave-safe bowl. Cover and cook on high 30-45 seconds or until warmed. Drizzle over the napoleons and sprinkle with peanuts. Serve immediately.

> Top layers of puff pastry and peanut butter ice cream with a warm, sweet drizzle the whole family will love! It's a terrific last-minute dessert. Or make them a day in advance and pop them in the freezer.
> —**JEANNE HOLT** MENDOTA HEIGHTS, MN

CHOCOLATE PEANUT CRUNCH ICE CREAM CAKE

People love this impressive-looking ice cream cake at family get-togethers! It's a favorite with adults and kids alike and it's easy to make. Enjoy!

—**KAREN EDWARDS** SANFORD, ME

PREP: 30 MIN. + FREEZING
MAKES: 14 SERVINGS

- 1 **cup milk chocolate chips**
- 2 **cups crushed Nutter Butter cookies (about 18 cookies)**
- 1 **quart vanilla ice cream, softened**
- 1 **quart chocolate ice cream, softened**
- 1 **cup heavy whipping cream**
- 1 **tablespoon confectioners' sugar**
- 1 **teaspoon vanilla extract**

1. In a small saucepan, melt chocolate chips over low heat. Stir in crushed cookies until coated. Spread on waxed paper to cool. Coarsely chop.
2. Spread vanilla ice cream into a 9-in. springform pan; sprinkle with 2 cups cookie mixture. Freeze for 30 minutes. Spread with chocolate ice cream. Cover and freeze 4 hours or until firm.
3. In a small bowl, beat cream until it begins to thicken. Add confectioners' sugar and vanilla; beat until stiff peaks form. Carefully run a knife around edge of pan to loosen. Remove sides of pan.
4. Spread whipped cream over top and sides of dessert; press remaining cookie mixture into sides. Freeze for 1 hour or until whipped cream is set. Remove ice cream cake from the freezer 15 minutes before serving.

NUTTY COOKIES & CREAM DESSERT

Flavors of hot fudge, caramel, chocolate cookies and ice cream all combine in every mouthful of this fabulous frozen dessert. No matter how big the meal, folks always find room for this treat!

—**CHERYL MELERSKI** HARBORCREEK, PA

PREP: 25 MIN. + FREEZING
MAKES: 15 SERVINGS

- 1 **package (15½ ounces) Oreo cookies, crushed**
- ½ **cup butter, melted**
- ½ **gallon cookies and cream ice cream, softened**
- 1½ **cups salted peanuts, coarsely chopped**
- ⅔ **cup hot fudge ice cream topping**
- ⅔ **cup caramel ice cream topping**
- 1 **carton (8 ounces) frozen whipped topping, thawed**

1. In a large bowl, combine cookie crumbs and butter; set aside 1 cup. Press remaining crumbs into an ungreased 13x9-in. dish. Spread with ice cream. Layer with peanuts, ice cream toppings and whipped topping; sprinkle with reserved crumbs. Cover and freeze until firm.
2. Remove from the freezer 15 minutes before serving.

WATERMELON BOMBE

I couldn't begin to count how many times I've made this wonderful dessert. It's a tradition at our summer barbecues. People go crazy for it, and yet it couldn't be easier. Love that!

—MARY ANN DELL PHOENIXVILLE, PA

PREP: 25 MIN. + FREEZING
MAKES: 8 SERVINGS

- 1 **pint pistachio ice cream, softened**
- 6 **drops green food coloring**
- 1 **pint vanilla ice cream, softened**
- 1 **pint strawberry ice cream, softened**
- 6 **drops red food coloring**
- ½ **cup miniature semisweet chocolate chips**

1. Line a 2-qt. freezer-safe bowl with plastic wrap. Place in the freezer for 30 minutes. In a small bowl, combine pistachio ice cream and green food coloring. Quickly spread pistachio ice cream over the bottom and up the sides to within ½ in. of the top of bowl. Freeze for 1 hour or until firm. Repeat with vanilla ice cream. Freeze 2 hours or until firm.

2. In a small bowl, combine strawberry ice cream and red food coloring; stir in chocolate chips. Spoon into ice cream shell. Cover and freeze overnight.

3. Remove from the freezer and invert onto a serving plate. Remove bowl and plastic wrap. Cut into wedges. Serve immediately.

COCONUT ICE CREAM TORTE

Guests will be impressed when you bring in this fabulous ice cream torte ringed with Almond Joy bars. The super-easy dessert feeds a crowd and can be made days ahead for convenience.

—TASTE OF HOME TEST KITCHEN

PREP: 15 MIN. + FREEZING
MAKES: 13 SERVINGS

- 18 **macaroons, crushed**
- ¼ **cup butter, melted**
- ¾ **cup hot fudge ice cream topping**
- 26 **snack-size Mounds or Almond Joy candy bars**
- 1 **quart vanilla ice cream, softened**
- 1 **quart strawberry ice cream, softened**
- ¼ **cup sliced almonds, toasted**

1. In a small bowl, combine cookie crumbs and butter. Press onto the bottom of a greased 10-in. springform pan. Freeze for 15 minutes.

2. In a microwave, heat hot fudge topping on high for 15-20 seconds or until pourable; spread over crust. Trim one end from each candy bar; arrange around edge of pan. Freeze 15 minutes. Spread vanilla ice cream over fudge topping; freeze for 30 minutes.

3. Spread strawberry ice cream over vanilla layer; sprinkle with almonds. Cover and freeze until firm. May be frozen for up to 2 months. Remove from the freezer 10 minutes before serving. Remove sides of pan.

NOTE *If Almond Joy candy bars are used, arrange bars with almond side facing inward toward the center of the pan.*

CARAMEL-MOCHA ICE CREAM DESSERT

You can use any flavor of ice cream in this frosty dessert. Chocolate and vanilla would be delicious substitutes for coffee and dulce de leche.

—SCARLETT ELROD NEWNAN, GA

PREP: 45 MIN. + FREEZING
MAKES: 20 SERVINGS

- 10 **whole graham crackers**
- 1 **cup butter, cubed**
- 1 **cup packed brown sugar**
- 1 **cup chopped pecans**

FILLING

- 1 **quart dulce de leche ice cream, softened**
- 1 **jar (16 ounces) hot fudge ice cream topping, warmed**
- 1 **quart coffee ice cream, softened**
- 1½ **cups heavy whipping cream**
- ⅓ **cup coffee liqueur**
    Chocolate curls

1. Preheat oven to 350°. Arrange crackers in a single layer in a greased 15x10x1-in. baking pan. In a large saucepan, melt butter over medium heat. Stir in brown sugar. Bring to a gentle boil; cook and stir for 2 minutes. Remove from the heat and stir in pecans. Pour over crackers; spread to cover crackers.
2. Bake 8-10 minutes or until bubbly. Cool completely on a wire rack.
3. Crush cracker mixture into coarse crumbs; sprinkle half into an ungreased 13x9-in. dish. Spread with dulce de leche ice cream. Cover and freeze for 1 hour or until firm.
4. Drizzle with ice cream topping and sprinkle with remaining crumb mixture. Cover and freeze 30 minutes or until ice cream topping is set.
5. Spread with coffee ice cream; freeze. In a small bowl, beat cream until stiff peaks form. Fold in coffee liqueur. Spread over top of dessert. Cover and freeze 4 hours or until firm.
6. Remove from freezer 15 minutes before serving. Garnish the top with chocolate curls.

CHOCOLATE TURTLE ICE CREAM PIE

Let the classic combination of chocolate, caramel and nuts wow your family and friends. They'd never believe how easy this irresistible pie is to make!

—MARGARET WILSON SUN CITY, CA

PREP: 15 MIN. + FREEZING
MAKES: 6-8 SERVINGS

- ¾ **cup small pecan halves, toasted**
- 6 **cups chocolate ice cream, softened**
- ½ **cup caramel ice cream topping, divided**
- 1 **graham cracker crust (9 inches)**
- ⅔ **cup whipped topping**

1. Set aside 12-16 pecan halves for garnish; chop remaining pecans. In a large bowl, combine the ice cream, ¼ cup caramel topping and chopped pecans. Spread into pie crust. Cover and freeze for at least 2½ hours.
2. Remove from the freezer 15 minutes before serving. Garnish with whipped topping, remaining caramel topping and reserved pecans.

RAINBOW SHERBET DESSERT

PREP: 30 MIN. + FREEZING • **MAKES:** 12 SERVINGS

- 12 **macaroon cookies, crumbled**
- 2 **cups heavy whipping cream**
- 3 **tablespoons confectioners' sugar**
- 1 **teaspoon vanilla extract**
- ¾ **cup chopped pecans, toasted**
- 1 **pint each raspberry, lime and orange sherbet, softened**

1. Preheat oven to 350°. Sprinkle cookie crumbs onto an ungreased baking sheet. Bake 5-8 minutes or until golden brown. Cool completely.

2. In a large bowl, beat cream until it begins to thicken. Add confectioners' sugar and vanilla; beat until stiff peaks form. Combine cookie crumbs and pecans; fold in whipped cream. Spread half of cream mixture onto the bottom of an ungreased 9-in. springform pan. Freeze 30 minutes.

3. Gently spread raspberry sherbet over cream layer. Layer with lime and orange sherbets; spread with remaining cream mixture. Cover and freeze until firm. Remove from the freezer 10 minutes before serving. Remove sides of pan.

Macaroons, pecans and layers of fruity sherbet combine in this special dessert. Try garnishing with fresh strawberries and just listen to folks "ooh" and "ahh" when you bring it in!

—**KATHRYN DUNN** AXTON, VA

Rainbow
Sherbet Dessert

CHOCOLATE DELIGHT DESSERT

My three children loved this dessert so much that they begged me to get the recipe. It's easy to make and tastes great. And preparing it ahead of time frees you up for other to-do's!

—**RUTH DYCK** FOREST, ON

PREP: 30 MIN. + FREEZING
MAKES: 12 SERVINGS

- 1 **cup crushed saltines**
- ½ **cup graham cracker crumbs**
- ⅓ **cup butter, melted**
- 2 **cups milk**
- 1 **package (3.9 ounces) instant chocolate pudding mix**
- 1 **package (3.4 ounces) instant vanilla pudding mix**
- 1½ **quarts cookies and cream ice cream, softened**
- 1 **carton (12 ounces) frozen whipped topping, thawed**
- 3 **Heath candy bars (1.4 ounces each), crushed**

1. In a small bowl, combine saltines and graham cracker crumbs; stir in butter. Press onto the bottom of a greased 13x9-in. baking pan. Refrigerate 15 minutes.

2. Meanwhile, in a large bowl, whisk milk and pudding mixes 2 minutes. Fold in ice cream. Spread over crust. Top with whipped topping; sprinkle with crushed candy bars. Freeze, covered, until firm. Remove from freezer 30 minutes before serving.

MUD PIE

We went to California more than 20 years ago and had this amazing pie at a restaurant. When I got home, I learned how to make it for my family. It's our favorite!

—SANDRA ASHCRAFT PUEBLO, CO

PREP: 25 MIN. + FREEZING
MAKES: 8 SERVINGS

- 1½ cups chocolate wafer crumbs
- ⅓ cup butter, melted
- 1 quart chocolate ice cream, softened
- 1 quart coffee ice cream, softened

CHOCOLATE SAUCE

- 2 tablespoons butter
- 2 ounces unsweetened chocolate
- 1 cup sugar
- ¼ teaspoon salt
- 1 can (5 ounces) evaporated milk
- ½ teaspoon vanilla extract

WHIPPED CREAM

- 1 cup heavy whipping cream
- 1 tablespoon sugar

1. Preheat oven to 350°. In a small bowl, combine wafer crumbs and butter. Press onto the bottom and up the sides of an ungreased 9-in. deep-dish pie plate. Bake 10 minutes. Cool on a wire rack.

2. In a large bowl, combine chocolate ice cream and coffee ice cream. Spoon into crust. Cover and freeze 8 hours or overnight.

3. For chocolate sauce, in a small saucepan, melt butter and chocolate over low heat; stir until smooth. Stir in sugar, salt and evaporated milk. Bring to a boil, stirring constantly. Remove from heat; stir in vanilla. Set aside.

4. Remove pie from the freezer 15 minutes before serving. In a small bowl, beat cream until it begins to thicken. Gradually add sugar; beat until soft peaks form.

5. Drizzle three stripes of chocolate sauce into a pastry bag; carefully add whipped cream. Pipe onto each slice of pie. Serve with remaining chocolate sauce.

MELTING CHOCOLATE

It's important to chop chocolate into uniform pieces to ensure even melting. Otherwise, the chocolate or chocolate mixture may burn before any large pieces have the chance to melt.

FROSTY NOTES

_____
_____
_____
_____
_____
_____
_____
_____
_____
_____
_____
_____
_____
_____
_____
_____
_____
_____
_____
_____
_____
_____
_____
_____
_____
_____
_____
_____
_____
_____
_____
_____
_____
_____
_____
_____
_____
_____

SMOOTH CHOCOLATE PIE

PREP: 25 MIN. + FREEZING • **MAKES:** 8 SERVINGS

- 1½ cups finely crushed chocolate wafers (about 24 wafers)
- ⅓ cup butter, melted
- 3 ounces cream cheese, softened
- 2 tablespoons sugar
- 4 ounces German sweet chocolate, melted
- ⅓ cup 2% milk
- 1 carton (8 ounces) frozen whipped topping, thawed
- Additional melted German sweet chocolate, optional

1. In a small bowl, mix wafer crumbs and melted butter. Press onto bottom and up sides of an ungreased 9-in. pie plate.

2. In a bowl, beat cream cheese and sugar until blended. Gradually beat in melted chocolate and milk. Refrigerate 10 minutes.

3. Fold whipped topping into chocolate mixture; spoon into crust. Freeze 4 hours or until firm. If desired, drizzle with melted chocolate before serving.

My mom and I made this chocolate pie, just the two of us, and our whole family got to enjoy it. We think you will, too.

—**STEVE RIEMERSMA** ALLEGAN, MI

Smooth Chocolate Pie

SHERBET CREAM CAKE

For an Easter ice cream social, it doesn't get any more show-stopping than this. In my family, this is how we celebrate special occasions and birthdays. It takes a little time to prepare, but it's easy and turns out beautifully and delicious!

—**PAULA WIPF** ARLINGTON, VA

PREP: 30 MIN. + FREEZING
MAKES: 14-16 SERVINGS

- 3 **cups each raspberry, orange and lime sherbet**
- 3 **quarts vanilla ice cream, softened, divided**
- 2 **cups chopped pecans, divided**
- 2 **cups miniature semisweet chocolate chips, divided**
- 3 **cups heavy whipping cream, whipped**
- 1 **pint fresh raspberries**
  Raspberries and orange and lime slices, optional

1. Using a ¼-cup ice cream scoop, shape sherbet into balls. Place on a waxed paper-lined baking sheet. Freeze for 1 hour or until firm.

2. In a large bowl, combine 1 qt. vanilla ice cream, 1 cup pecans and 1 cup chocolate chips. Spread into a 10-in. tube pan.

3. Alternately arrange 12 sherbet balls, four of each color, against the center tube and outer edge of pan. Freeze for 30 minutes.

4. Spread with 1 qt. ice cream; freeze for 30 minutes. Top with remaining sherbet balls. Combine remaining ice cream, pecans and chips; spread over sherbet balls. Freeze overnight.

5. Run a knife around edge of pan; dip pan in lukewarm water until loosened. Invert cake onto a serving plate. Frost with whipped cream. Return to freezer. Remove from freezer 10 minutes before serving. Garnish with fruit if desired.

NUTTY CARAMEL ICE CREAM CAKE

Tuck this dessert in the freezer for one of those anytime celebrations. This caramel, butter pecan and almond version is our favorite, but try it with other ice cream flavors.

—DAVID STELZL WAXHAW, NC

PREP: 30 MIN. + FREEZING
MAKES: 16 SERVINGS

- 4 **cups crushed pecan shortbread cookies (about 52 cookies)**
- ¼ **cup butter, melted**
- 6 **cups butter pecan ice cream, softened**
- 1 **carton (8 ounces) frozen whipped topping, thawed**
- ¾ **cup slivered almonds, toasted**
- ¾ **cup milk chocolate English toffee bits**
- ¼ **cup caramel sundae syrup**

1. In a large bowl, combine cookie crumbs and butter. Press 2 cups onto the bottom of a greased 9-in. springform pan. Spoon half of the ice cream into the prepared pan. Freeze for 20 minutes.

2. Repeat layers with remaining cookie crumbs and ice cream. Spread with whipped topping. Sprinkle with almonds and toffee bits. Cover and freeze overnight or until firm. May be frozen for up to 2 months.

TO USE FROZEN CAKE *Remove from the freezer 10 minutes before serving. Drizzle with syrup.*

MINT-CHOCOLATE ICE CREAM CAKE

This ice cream cake is so easy to make and terrific for special occasions!

—KATHY MORROW HUBBARD, OH

PREP: 15 MIN. + FREEZING
MAKES: 10 SERVINGS

- 2 **packages (10 ounces each) individual cream-filled chocolate cakes**
- 3 **cups mint chocolate chip ice cream, softened**
- 12 **Oreo cookies, crushed, divided**
- 2 **cups whipped topping**
- ½ **teaspoon mint extract, optional**

1. Line a 9x5-in. loaf pan with plastic wrap. Place six cakes in pan, completely covering bottom. Spread ice cream over top; sprinkle with half of the cookie crumbs. Press remaining cakes on top. Freeze at least 3 hours.

2. Just before serving, remove from the freezer and invert onto a serving plate. Remove pan and plastic wrap.

3. Combine whipped topping and extract if desired; frost top and sides of cake. Sprinkle with remaining crumbs.

NOTE *This recipe was tested with Little Debbie Devil Cremes.*

FROZEN BANANA SPLIT PIE

This dessert is special enough to turn hamburgers and fries into a meal to remember! It's tall and pretty, and tastes just like a frozen banana split. Make it ahead to save time.

—JOY COLLINS BIRMINGHAM, AL

PREP: 25 MIN. + FREEZING
MAKES: 8 SERVINGS

- 3 **tablespoons chocolate hard-shell ice cream topping**
- 1 **graham cracker crust (9 inches)**
- 2 **medium bananas, sliced**
- ½ **teaspoon lemon juice**
- ½ **cup pineapple ice cream topping**
- 1 **quart strawberry ice cream, softened**
- 2 **cups whipped topping**
- ½ **cup chopped walnuts, toasted Chocolate syrup**
- 8 **maraschino cherries with stems**

1. Pour chocolate topping into crust; freeze for 5 minutes or until chocolate is firm.

2. Meanwhile, place bananas in a small bowl; toss with lemon juice. Arrange bananas over chocolate topping. Layer with pineapple topping, ice cream, whipped topping and walnuts.

3. Cover and freeze until firm. Remove from the freezer 15 minutes before cutting. Garnish with chocolate syrup and cherries.

LEMONADE DESSERT

Here's a tasty way to finish off your summer barbecue. Adults and kids will be standing in line for this easy-to-make treat.

—MARGARET LINDER QUINCY, WA

PREP: 30 MIN. + FREEZING
MAKES: 12-15 SERVINGS

- 1½ **cups all-purpose flour**
- ¾ **cup packed brown sugar**
- ¾ **cup cold butter, cubed**
- ¾ **cup chopped pecans**
- ½ **gallon vanilla ice cream, softened**
- 1 **can (12 ounces) frozen lemonade concentrate, thawed**

1. Preheat oven to 375°. In a small bowl, combine flour and brown sugar; cut in butter until crumbly. Stir in pecans. Spread in a single layer into a greased 15x10x1-in. baking pan.

2. Bake 9-12 minutes or until golden brown, stirring once. Cool on a wire rack 10 minutes.

3. In a large bowl, beat ice cream and lemonade until blended. Sprinkle half of the crumbles into a greased 13x9-in. dish. Spread with ice cream mixture; sprinkle with remaining crumbles. Cover and freeze overnight. Remove dessert from the freezer 15 minutes before serving.

Spumoni Baked Alaska

SPUMONI BAKED ALASKA

For a refreshing end to a special meal, try this freezer finale.

—TASTE OF HOME TEST KITCHEN

PREP: 50 MIN. + FREEZING • **BAKE:** 5 MIN.
MAKES: 12 SERVINGS

- ½ **cup butter, cubed**
- 2 **ounces unsweetened chocolate, chopped**
- 1 **cup sugar**
- 1 **teaspoon vanilla extract**
- 2 **eggs**
- ¾ **cup all-purpose flour**
- ½ **teaspoon baking powder**
- ½ **teaspoon salt**
- 1 **cup chopped hazelnuts**
- 2 **quarts vanilla ice cream, softened, divided**
- ½ **cup chopped pistachios**
- ½ **teaspoon almond extract**
- 6 **drops green food coloring, optional**
- ⅓ **cup chopped maraschino cherries**
- 1 **tablespoon maraschino cherry juice**
- 1 **tablespoon rum**

MERINGUE

- 8 **egg whites**
- 1 **cup sugar**
- 1 **teaspoon cream of tartar**

1. Preheat oven to 350°. In a microwave-safe bowl, melt butter and chocolate; stir until smooth. Stir in sugar and vanilla. Add eggs, one at a time, beating well after each addition. Combine the flour, baking powder and salt; gradually stir into chocolate mixture. Stir in hazelnuts.

2. Spread into a greased 8-in. round baking pan. Bake 35-40 minutes or until a toothpick inserted near the center comes out with moist crumbs (do not overbake). Cool 10 minutes before removing from pan to a wire rack to cool completely.

3. Meanwhile, line an 8-in. round bowl (1½ qts.) with foil. In a small bowl, place 1 qt. ice cream; add pistachios, almond extract and food coloring if desired. Quickly spread ice cream over bottom and up sides of bowl, leaving center hollow; cover and freeze 30 minutes.

4. In a small bowl, combine cherries, cherry juice, rum and remaining ice cream. Pack ice cream into center; cover and freeze.

5. In a large heavy saucepan, combine egg whites, sugar and cream of tartar. With a hand mixer, beat on low speed 1 minute. Continue beating over low heat until egg mixture reaches 160°, about 8 minutes. Transfer to a bowl; beat until stiff glossy peaks form and sugar is dissolved.

6. Place brownie on an ungreased foil-lined baking sheet; top with inverted ice cream mold. Remove foil. Spread meringue over ice cream, sealing to edges of brownie. Freeze until ready to serve, up to 24 hours.

7. Preheat oven to 400°. Bake 2-5 minutes or until meringue is lightly browned. Transfer to a serving plate; serve immediately.

BEST MERINGUE

Even a trace amount of fat can keep a meringue from reaching its maximum volume. Make sure the bowl, pan and beaters are very clean, and that the egg whites contain no bits of yolk.

_____
_____
_____
_____
_____
_____
_____
_____
_____
_____
_____
_____
_____
_____
_____
_____
_____
_____
_____
_____
_____
_____
_____
_____
_____
_____
_____
_____
_____
_____
_____
_____
_____
_____
_____
_____
_____
_____
_____
_____
_____
_____

ICE CREAM COOKIE DESSERT

Our family loves dessert, and this chocolaty layered treat is one of Mom's most-requested recipes.
—KIMBERLY LAABS HARTFORD, WI

PREP: 15 MIN. + FREEZING • **MAKES:** 12 SERVINGS

- 1 **package (15½ ounces) Oreo cookies**
- ¼ **cup butter, melted**
- ½ **gallon vanilla ice cream, softened**
- 1 **jar (16 ounces) hot fudge ice cream topping, warmed**
- 1 **carton (8 ounces) frozen whipped topping, thawed**

1. In a large bowl, combine 3¾ cups cookie crumbs and butter. Press into a greased 13x9-in. dish. Spread with ice cream; cover and freeze until set.

2. Drizzle fudge topping over ice cream; cover and freeze until set. Spread with whipped topping; sprinkle with remaining cookie crumbs. Cover and freeze 2 hours or until firm. Remove from the freezer 10 minutes before serving.

TOFFEE COFFEE ICE CREAM

Need an afternoon pick-me-up? Try this rich ice cream treat that's loaded with sweet and crunchy goodies. It'll make the rest of the day a little sweeter.
—TASTE OF HOME TEST KITCHEN

START TO FINISH: 10 MIN. • **MAKES:** 5 SERVINGS

- 1 **pint coffee ice cream, softened**
- ¼ **cup miniature marshmallows**
- ¼ **cup milk chocolate-covered almonds, halved**
- 1 **English toffee candy bar, chopped**

In a large bowl, stir the ice cream, marshmallows, chocolate-covered almonds and chopped candy bar until blended. Serve immediately.

Ice Cream
Cookie Dessert

Orange Whipped
Dessert

ORANGE WHIPPED DESSERT

It takes only minutes to blend together this cool, silky treat. The yogurt adds refreshing tanginess. It's refreshing on warm summer days.

—SUE THOMAS CASA GRANDE, AZ

PREP: 10 MIN. + FREEZING
MAKES: 4 SERVINGS

- 1 **can (11 ounces) mandarin oranges, drained and patted dry**
- 1 **cup (8 ounces) vanilla yogurt**
- 2 **tablespoons thawed orange juice concentrate**
- 2 **cups whipped topping**

In a large bowl, combine the oranges, yogurt and orange juice concentrate. Fold in whipped topping. Spoon into serving dishes. Cover and freeze until firm. Remove from freezer 10 minutes before serving.

FROZEN LEMONADE SQUARES

Mom always made this special treat when the weather started to get warm. Whenever I see the temperature start to climb I make sure I have one in the freezer.

—KARA O'REILLY PORTLAND, OR

PREP: 15 MIN. + FREEZING
MAKES: 2 DOZEN

- 1⅓ **cups graham cracker crumbs**
- ⅔ **cup crushed vanilla wafers (about 18 wafers)**
- ½ **cup sugar**
- ½ **cup butter, melted**
- 2 **quarts vanilla ice cream, softened**
- ¾ **cup thawed pink lemonade concentrate**

1. In a small bowl, mix cracker crumbs, wafer crumbs and sugar; stir in butter. Reserve ¼ cup for topping. Press remaining crumb mixture onto bottom of a greased 13x9-in. baking pan.
2. In a large bowl, mix ice cream and lemonade concentrate. Spread over crust; top with reserved crumb mixture. Freeze overnight or until firm.

BLUEBERRY ICE CREAM TART

Absolutely no one will believe how easy this beautiful treat is to make! The quick crust boasts just a hint of cinnamon. It's a simply wonderful summer dessert.

—SHIRLEY FOLTZ DEXTER, KS

PREP: 15 MIN. + FREEZING
MAKES: 12 SERVINGS

- 1½ **cups crushed vanilla wafers (about 45 wafers)**
- 1 **teaspoon ground cinnamon**
- ⅓ **cup butter, melted**
- 1 **quart vanilla ice cream, softened**
- 1 **can (21 ounces) blueberry pie filling**

1. In a small bowl, combine wafer crumbs and cinnamon; stir in butter. Press onto the bottom of a greased 9-in. springform pan; set aside.
2. Place ice cream in a large bowl; gently fold in pie filling. Spread over crust. Cover and freeze until firm. Remove from the freezer 10 minutes before serving. Remove sides of pan.

FROZEN RASPBERRY CHEESECAKES

PREP: 15 MIN. + FREEZING
MAKES: 2 SERVINGS

- ½ **cup crushed shortbread cookies**
- 2 **tablespoons butter, melted**
- 3 **ounces cream cheese, softened**
- ⅓ **cup sweetened condensed milk**
- 2 **tablespoons lemon juice**
- ⅔ **cup raspberry sherbet, softened**
  Fresh raspberries

1. In a small bowl, combine cookie crumbs and butter. Press onto the bottom of two 4-in. springform pans coated with cooking spray. Freeze 10 minutes. In a small bowl, beat the cream cheese, milk and lemon juice until blended. Spread over crust. Freeze 2 hours or until firm.
2. Spread sherbet over tops; freeze 2 hours longer. Top with raspberries.

With the delectable taste of raspberry cheesecake ice cream, this dessert is an elegant ending to any meal. A friend from church originally made a version with lime sherbet. I loved the taste, but this is a pretty variation with berries.
—VICKI MELIES ELKHORN, NE

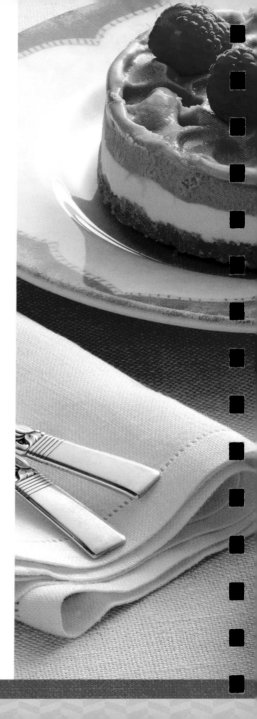

Frosty Raspberry
Cheesecakes

Hazelnut
Brownie Bombe

HAZELNUT BROWNIE BOMBE

I love to make ice cream bombes. They look elegant yet are incredibly simple to create.
—MELISSA MILLWOOD LYMAN, SC

PREP: 45 MIN. • **BAKE:** 55 MIN. + FREEZING
MAKES: 16 SERVINGS

- 2 **cups (12 ounces) semisweet chocolate chips**
- ½ **cup butter, cubed**
- 3 **eggs**
- 1½ **cups sugar**
- ½ **teaspoon salt**
- 1 **teaspoon vanilla extract**
- ¾ **cup all-purpose flour**
- 3 **cups whole hazelnuts, toasted and chopped, divided**
- 3 **quarts chocolate ice cream, softened if necessary**
- ½ **cup Nutella**

1. Preheat oven to 350°. Line bottom of a greased 9-in. springform pan with parchment paper; grease paper.

2. In a microwave, melt chocolate chips and butter; stir until smooth. Cool slightly. In a large bowl, beat eggs, sugar and salt. Stir in vanilla and chocolate mixture. Add flour, mixing well. Stir in 1 cup hazelnuts.

3. Spread batter into the prepared pan. Bake 55-60 minutes or until a toothpick inserted in center comes out with moist crumbs (do not overbake). Cool completely in pan on a wire rack.

4. Meanwhile, line a 4-qt. bowl with a 9-in.-diameter top with plastic wrap. Quickly spread ice cream into bowl. Freeze, covered, until firm.

5. Loosen sides of brownie with a knife; remove rim from pan. Transfer brownie to a serving plate and remove paper. Spread top with Nutella. Invert ice cream mold onto brownie; remove bowl and plastic wrap. Immediately press remaining hazelnuts onto ice cream. Freeze, covered, at least 1 hour before serving. Cut brownie bombe into wedges.

FROSTY NOTES

CHERRY ICE CREAM CAKE

A friend shared this recipe, which has become an all-time favorite of mine.
—**KATHY KITTELL** LENEXA, KS

PREP: 20 MIN. + FREEZING
MAKES: 12 SERVINGS (1¼ CUPS SAUCE)

- ⅔ **cup heavy whipping cream**
- 2 **tablespoons butter**
- 1 **package (11 ounces) milk chocolate chips**
- 1 **teaspoon vanilla extract**

ICE CREAM CAKE
- 2 **pints cherry or cherry vanilla ice cream, softened, divided**
- 3 **cups crushed shortbread cookies, divided**
- 1 **pint vanilla ice cream, softened**

1. In a small saucepan, heat cream and butter over low heat until butter is melted; remove from the heat. Add chips; let stand for 1 minute. Whisk until sauce is smooth. Stir in vanilla. Cool 30 minutes, stirring occasionally.
2. Meanwhile, line the bottom and sides of a 9x5-in. loaf pan with plastic wrap. Spread 1 pint cherry ice cream into prepared pan; sprinkle with 1 cup cookie crumbs. Top with vanilla ice cream. Freeze 20 minutes or until firm.
3. Spread with ¾ cup chocolate sauce; freeze 20 minutes. Top with remaining cherry ice cream; sprinkle with 1 cup cookie crumbs. Cover and freeze 4 hours. Transfer remaining sauce to a microwave-safe dish; refrigerate.
4. Remove dessert from freezer 10 minutes before serving. Using plastic wrap, remove dessert from pan; discard plastic wrap. Press remaining cookie crumbs into sides. Using a serrated knife, cut into slices. Microwave reserved sauce; serve with dessert.

FROSTY ALMOND DESSERT

You can treat your family to a homemade dessert without a lot of work when you whip up this confection. Everyone will love its yummy flavor.
—**PHYLLIS SCHMALZ** KANSAS CITY, KS

START TO FINISH: 10 MIN.
MAKES: 4 SERVINGS

- 4 **cups low-fat vanilla frozen yogurt**
- 1 **cup ice cubes**
- ½ **cup hot fudge ice cream topping**
- ¼ **teaspoon almond extract**
  Whipped topping and baking cocoa, optional

1. In a blender, place half of the yogurt, ice cubes, fudge topping and extract; cover and process for 1-2 minutes or until smooth. Stir if necessary. Pour into chilled dessert glasses.
2. Repeat with remaining yogurt, ice, fudge topping and extract. Garnish with whipped topping and cocoa if desired.

PEANUT BUTTER-CHOCOLATE ICE CREAM TORTE

What's not to love about peanut butter, chocolate, ice cream and Oreo cookies? This fancy frozen dessert is a cinch to put together. What a great dessert to have on hand for unexpected guests this summer!

—**DANA SOUTHWICK** MANTON, CA

PREP: 30 MIN. + FREEZING
MAKES: 12 SERVINGS

- 24 **Oreo cookies**
- ⅓ **cup butter, melted**

FILLING

- 1 **quart chocolate ice cream, softened**
- 1½ **cups creamy peanut butter**
- 1 **quart peanut butter ice cream with peanut butter cup pieces, softened**

TOPPING

- 2 **cups (12 ounces) semisweet chocolate chips**
- 1 **cup heavy whipping cream**
- 1½ **cups coarsely chopped miniature peanut butter cups**

1. Place cookies in a food processor. Cover and pulse until fine crumbs form. Transfer to a large bowl and stir in butter. Press onto the bottom and 1 in. up the sides of a greased 10-in. springform pan; cover and freeze for at least 15 minutes.

2. Spread chocolate ice cream into crust; cover and freeze until firm. Spread peanut butter over chocolate layer and top with peanut butter ice cream. Cover and freeze until firm.

3. Place chocolate chips in a large bowl. In a small saucepan, bring cream just to a boil. Pour over chocolate; whisk until smooth. Cool to room temperature, stirring occasionally. Spread over top of dessert. Immediately sprinkle with peanut butter cups. Cover and freeze for 1 hour before serving.

CREATE A FLAVOR

Use your imagination with this pie. Combine Golden Oreos with butter brickle ice cream, Mint Oreos with mint chip ice cream or Berry Oreos with berry ice cream.

Cookie Ice Cream Pie

COOKIE ICE CREAM PIE

PREP: 25 MIN. + FREEZING
MAKES: 8 SERVINGS

- 10 **Oreo cookies, finely crushed**
- 3 **tablespoons butter, melted**
- 14 **whole Oreo cookies**

FILLING

- ½ **gallon raspberry ripple ice cream, softened, divided**
- ½ **cup prepared fudge topping, divided**
  Fresh raspberries, optional

1. In a small bowl, combine crushed cookies and butter. Press onto bottom of a 9-in. pie plate. Stand whole cookies up around edges, pressing lightly into crust. Freeze 1 hour or until set.

2. For filling, spread half of ice cream over crushed cookies. Drizzle with ¼ cup of fudge topping. Freeze 1 hour or until set.

3. Spread remaining ice cream on top. Drizzle with remaining fudge topping. Freeze several hours or overnight.

4. Garnish with fresh raspberries if desired. Let stand at room temperature for 15 minutes before cutting.

> This crunchy, creamy treat won't heat up your kitchen on sweltering days. Whip it up for company or the neighborhood kids.
> **—DEBBIE WALSH** MADISON, WI

STRAWBERRY ICE CREAM CHARLOTTE

My family loves ice cream cake, so all were delighted when I introduced them to this tasty dessert.
—SCARLETT ELROD NEWNAN, GA

PREP: 35 MIN. + FREEZING
MAKES: 12 SLICES

- 2 **packages (3 ounces each) soft ladyfingers, split**
- 4 **cups strawberry ice cream, softened if necessary**
- 1¾ **cups strawberry sorbet, softened if necessary**
- 2 **cups fresh strawberries, hulled**
- 2 **tablespoons confectioners' sugar**
- ¾ **cup marshmallow creme**
- 1 **cup heavy whipping cream**

1. Line the sides and bottom of an ungreased 9-in. springform pan with ladyfingers, rounded sides out; trim to fit if necessary. (Save remaining ladyfingers for another use.)

2. Quickly spread ice cream into pan; freeze, covered, 30 minutes. Spread sorbet over the ice cream; freeze 30 minutes longer.

3. Meanwhile, place strawberries and confectioners' sugar in a food processor; process until pureed. Reserve ¼ cup puree for swirling. Transfer remaining puree to a large bowl; whisk in the marshmallow creme.

4. In a small bowl, beat cream until soft peaks form. Fold into marshmallow mixture. Spread evenly over sorbet; drizzle with reserved puree. Cut through puree with a knife to swirl. Freeze, covered, overnight.

5. Remove from freezer; carefully loosen sides of pan with a knife. Remove rim from pan. Serve immediately.

CHERRY LINCOLN LOG

I first made this festive cake roll to celebrate Lincoln's birthday, but it's a great dessert for any holiday or special meal.

—MARILYN JENSEN CODY, WY

PREP: 30 MIN. • **BAKE:** 10 MIN. + FREEZING
MAKES: 14 SERVINGS

- 3 **eggs**
- 1 **cup sugar**
- 1/3 **cup water**
- 1 **teaspoon vanilla extract**
- 1 **cup all-purpose flour**
- 1/3 **cup baking cocoa**
- 1 **teaspoon baking powder**
- 1/4 **teaspoon salt**
   Confectioners' sugar
- 1 **quart cherry ice cream, softened**

FROSTING

- 1 **ounce unsweetened chocolate**
- 1 **tablespoon butter**
- 1 1/4 **cups confectioners' sugar**
- 2 **to 3 tablespoons milk**

1. Preheat oven to 375°. Line a greased 15x10x1-in. baking pan with waxed paper; grease the paper and set aside. In a large bowl, beat eggs 3 minutes. Gradually add sugar; beat 2 minutes or until thick and lemon-colored. Beat in water and vanilla. Combine flour, cocoa, baking powder and salt; fold into egg mixture (batter will be thin).

2. Spread into prepared pan. Bake 10-13 minutes or until cake springs back when lightly touched. Cool 5 minutes. Invert onto a kitchen towel dusted with confectioners' sugar. Gently peel off waxed paper. Roll up cake in the towel jelly-roll style, starting with a short side. Cool completely on a wire rack.

3. For frosting, in microwave-safe bowl, melt chocolate and butter; stir until smooth. Gradually beat in confectioners' sugar and enough milk to achieve desired consistency.

4. Unroll cake; spread ice cream evenly over cake to within 1/2 in. of edges. Roll up again. Place seam side down on a serving platter. Spread with frosting. Cover and freeze overnight.

BERRY CASHEW ICE CREAM

Lots of fresh berries and crunchy nuts make this ice cream loads of fun.

—TASTE OF HOME TEST KITCHEN

START TO FINISH: 10 MIN.
MAKES: 5 SERVINGS

- 2 **cups French vanilla ice cream, softened**
- 1/4 **cup salted cashews**
- 1/4 **cup fresh raspberries**
- 1/4 **cup fresh blueberries**
- 1 **tablespoon miniature semisweet chocolate chips**
- 1 **tablespoon caramel ice cream topping**
- 1 **individual graham cracker tart shell, broken into large pieces**

Combine first six ingredients. Gently fold in graham cracker pieces. Serve immediately.

MEXICAN ICE CREAM

I made this ice cream for my grandma and her friends, and they loved it. This simple, flavorful dessert is a perfect way to get kids involved in the kitchen.

—**BEN PHIPPS** LIMA, OH

PREP: 20 MIN. + FREEZING
MAKES: 4 SERVINGS

- 2 **cups vanilla ice cream**
- ½ **cup frosted cornflakes, crushed**
- ¼ **cup sugar**
- 1 **teaspoon ground cinnamon**
- ¼ **cup honey**

1. Place four ½-cup scoops of ice cream on a waxed paper-lined baking sheet. Freeze for 1 hour or until firm.

2. In a shallow bowl, combine the cornflake crumbs, sugar and cinnamon. Roll ice cream in crumb mixture to coat. Freeze until serving. Drizzle each serving with 1 tablespoon honey.

CHILLY
SANDWICHES

HONEY-BANANA ICE CREAM SANDWICHES

As busy as the summer season is, you'll want to take a little time to make these yummy frozen confections. The cool, sweet filling between chocolate graham crackers is irresistible to everyone.

—SUSAN ASANOVIC WILTON, CT

PREP: 1 HOUR + FREEZING • **MAKES:** 10 SERVINGS

- 1 **cup whole milk**
- ½ **cup sugar**
- ⅓ **cup honey**
- 2 **ripe medium bananas**
- 2 **cups heavy whipping cream, divided**
- 1½ **teaspoons vanilla extract**
- ¼ **teaspoon almond extract**
- ⅛ **teaspoon salt**
- ½ **cup dried banana chips, chopped**
- 10 **whole chocolate graham crackers, halved**
- ¾ **cup finely chopped salted peanuts**
- ¼ **cup chocolate jimmies**

1. In a small heavy saucepan, heat the milk and sugar until bubbles form around the sides of pan. Whisk in the honey. Quickly transfer to a large bowl; place in ice water and stir 2 minutes.

2. Puree bananas; add to cooled milk mixture with 1 cup cream, extracts and salt. Press waxed paper onto surface of milk mixture. Refrigerate for several hours or overnight.

3. In a small bowl, beat remaining cream until soft peaks form; fold into banana mixture. Fill the cylinder of ice cream freezer two-thirds full; freeze according to manufacturer's directions, adding the banana chips during the last minute. When ice cream is frozen, transfer to a freezer container; freeze for 2-4 hours.

4. To assemble sandwiches, spread ice cream onto each of 10 graham cracker halves. Top with remaining graham crackers; press down gently.

5. In a shallow dish, combine the peanuts and jimmies. Roll the sides of ice cream sandwiches in peanut mixture. Wrap in plastic wrap; freeze on a baking sheet at least 1 hour.

FROSTY NOTES

PEANUT BUTTER ICE CREAM SANDWICHES

Store-bought ice cream treats just can't compare to homemade ones. These are fantastic!

—TERESA GAETZKE NORTH FREEDOM, WI

PREP: 45 MIN. • **BAKE:** 10 MIN. + FREEZING
MAKES: 16 SERVINGS

- ½ **cup shortening**
- ½ **cup creamy peanut butter**
- ¾ **cup sugar, divided**
- ½ **cup packed brown sugar**
- 1 **egg**
- ½ **teaspoon vanilla extract**
- 1½ **cups all-purpose flour**
- 1 **teaspoon baking soda**
- ½ **teaspoon salt**
- 12 **ounces dark chocolate candy coating, chopped**
- 1 **quart vanilla ice cream, softened**

1. Preheat oven to 350°. In a large bowl, cream the shortening, peanut butter, ½ cup sugar and brown sugar until light and fluffy. Beat in egg and vanilla. Combine the flour, baking soda and salt; gradually add to creamed mixture and mix well.

2. Roll the cookie dough into 1-in. balls; roll in remaining sugar. Place 1 in. apart on ungreased baking sheets. Flatten with a fork, forming a crisscross pattern.

3. Bake 9-11 minutes or until the cookies are set (do not overbake). Remove to wire racks to cool completely.

4. In a microwave, melt the candy coating; stir until smooth. Spread a heaping teaspoonful on the bottom of each cookie; place chocolate side up on waxed paper until set.

5. To make ice cream sandwiches, place ¼ cup ice cream on the bottom of half of the cookies; top with remaining cookies. Wrap in plastic wrap; freeze on a baking sheet overnight.

Peanut Butter
Ice Cream Sandwiches

CHOCOLATE ICE CREAM SANDWICHES

I love surprising my family with extra-special desserts, especially frosty ones on hot days. Plain vanilla ice cream lets my homemade double-chocolate cookies take center stage.

—MICHELLE WOLFORD SAN ANTONIO, TX

PREP: 20 MIN. • **BAKE:** 10 MIN. + COOLING
MAKES: 8 SERVINGS

- ⅓ **cup butter, softened**
- ⅓ **cup sugar**
- ⅓ **cup packed brown sugar**
- 1 **egg**
- ½ **teaspoon vanilla extract**
- ¾ **cup plus 2 tablespoons all-purpose flour**
- ¼ **cup baking cocoa**
- ½ **teaspoon baking powder**
- ¼ **teaspoon baking soda**
- ¼ **teaspoon salt**
- ½ **cup semisweet chocolate chips**
- 1 **pint vanilla ice cream**

1. Preheat oven to 375°. In a large bowl, cream butter and sugars until light and fluffy. Beat in egg and vanilla. Combine the flour, cocoa, baking powder, baking soda and salt; add to creamed mixture and mix well.

2. Drop by rounded tablespoonfuls 2 in. apart onto greased baking sheets, forming 16 cookies. Flatten slightly with a glass. Sprinkle with chocolate chips. Bake 8-10 minutes or until set. Remove to wire racks to cool.

3. To make ice cream sandwiches, spread ¼ cup vanilla ice cream on the bottoms of half of the cookies; cover with the remaining cookies. Wrap each in plastic wrap; freeze on a baking sheet overnight.

RASPBERRY-ORANGE ICE CREAM SANDWICHES

These sorbet treats get a hint of citrus from the orange peel stirred into the brownies.
—*TASTE OF HOME* **TEST KITCHEN**

PREP: 25 MIN. • **BAKE:** 10 MIN. + FREEZING
MAKES: 12-15 SERVINGS

> **Brownie for Ice Cream Sandwiches (recipe on page 152)**
> ½ to 1 teaspoon grated orange peel
> 4 cups raspberry sorbet, softened
> 1 package (10 ounces) frozen sweetened raspberries, thawed and drained
> White chocolate curls, optional

1. Prepare batter for Brownie for Ice Cream Sandwiches; stir in peel. Bake and cool according to recipe directions.
2. Cut the brownie in half widthwise. In a bowl, stir the sorbet and berries together. Spread the sorbet mixture over one brownie half. Turn over the remaining brownie half; place over sorbet. Cover and freeze on a baking sheet 2 hours or until firm.
3. Cut into bars, squares or desired shapes. Dip the sides of the ice cream sandwiches in white chocolate curls if desired. Wrap in plastic wrap; freeze until serving.

> ### BROWNIE BEST
>
> Raspberry-Orange Ice Cream Sandwiches (above) and two other recipes in this chapter use the Brownie for Ice Cream Sandwiches recipe on page 152.

SICILIAN ICE CREAM SANDWICHES

Indulge in a taste of Italy! Rich Nutella, chocolate, pistachios and cherries come together for a sweet sensation.
—**MATTHEW HASS** FRANKLIN, WI

PREP: 20 MIN. + FREEZING
MAKES: 4 SERVINGS

> 1 teaspoon shortening
> ⅔ cup miniature semisweet chocolate chips, divided
> 4 miniature croissants, split
> ¼ cup Nutella
> 4 scoops pistachio gelato
> 12 maraschino cherries, divided
> ⅓ cup pistachios, coarsely chopped

1. In a microwave, melt shortening and ⅓ cup chocolate chips; stir until smooth. Set aside.
2. Toast the croissants. Spread the cut sides of croissants with Nutella. Place a scoop of gelato on croissant bottoms. Slice eight cherries; arrange over gelato. Replace croissant tops.

GIANT PEANUT BUTTER ICE CREAM SANDWICH

I created this for my husband, adding light and reduced-fat products to convenient refrigerated cookie dough. When we have guests, I make the recipe using conventional ingredients—feel free to go either way!

—**JOANN BELACK** BRADENTON, FL

PREP: 30 MIN. • **BAKE:** 20 MIN. + FREEZING
MAKES: 12 SERVINGS

- 2 packages (16 ounces each) ready-to-bake refrigerated peanut butter cup cookie dough
- 6 whole chocolate graham crackers, crushed
- 1 cup cold milk
- 1 cup heavy whipping cream
- 1 package (3.4 ounces) instant vanilla pudding mix
- 1 package (8 ounces) cream cheese, softened
- 1⅓ cups creamy peanut butter
- 3 cups vanilla ice cream, softened
- ¼ cup Nutella

1. Preheat oven to 350°. Let the peanut butter cup cookie dough stand at room temperature 5-10 minutes to soften. Press the softened cookie dough into two ungreased 9-in. springform pans; sprinkle with the chocolate graham cracker crumbs. Bake 20-25 minutes or until set. Cool completely.

2. In a large bowl, whisk the cold milk, heavy whipping cream and pudding mix 2 minutes. Let stand 2 minutes until soft-set. In another large bowl, beat the cream cheese and peanut butter until smooth. Add the pudding and vanilla ice cream; beat until smooth.

3. Spread the ice cream mixture over one cookie crust. Remove the sides of the second pan; place the cookie crust, crumb side down, over filling. Wrap in plastic wrap; freeze on a baking sheet 4 hours or until firm.

4. Remove from freezer 15 minutes before serving. Place the Nutella in a small microwave-safe bowl; cover and microwave at 50% power 1-2 minutes or until smooth, stirring twice. Remove the sides of pan; cut dessert into slices. Drizzle with Nutella.

COOL & CREAMY ICE CREAM SANDWICHES

Here's an unusual but amazingly good combination of strawberry ice cream and jalapeno peppers. It's a grown-up version of a classic summer favorite.

—**MELISSA HANSEN** ROCHESTER, MN

PREP: 20 MIN. + FREEZING
MAKES: 4 SERVINGS

- 6 tablespoons chopped seeded jalapeno peppers
- 4 teaspoons butter
- ¼ cup jalapeno pepper jelly
- 8 soft snickerdoodle cookies
- 4 scoops strawberry ice cream
- 4 fresh strawberries, hulled and sliced

1. In a small skillet, saute the jalapeno peppers in butter until tender. Add jelly; set aside to cool.

2. To make the ice cream sandwiches, place a scoop of strawberry ice cream on bottom of half of the snickerdoodle cookies. Top with fresh strawberries, jalapeno pepper mixture and remaining snickerdoodle cookies. Wrap each sandwich in plastic wrap; freeze on a baking sheet overnight.

NOTE *Wear disposable gloves when cutting hot peppers; the oils can burn skin. Avoid touching your face.*

Giant Peanut Butter
Ice Cream Sandwich

Gingerbread Ice
Cream Sandwiches

When it comes to ice cream sandwiches, not all gingerbread men are created equal! Some are too crispy while others are too soft. But these thin yet sturdy boys hold up well in the freezer.

—*TASTE OF HOME* TEST KITCHEN

GINGERBREAD ICE CREAM SANDWICHES

PREP: 30 MIN. + CHILLING
BAKE: 10 MIN./BATCH + FREEZING
MAKES: 12 SERVINGS

> 3 **cups vanilla ice cream**
> ¾ **teaspoon ground cinnamon**
> **COOKIES**
> ⅓ **cup butter, softened**
> ½ **cup packed brown sugar**
> 1 **egg**
> ⅓ **cup molasses**
> 2 **cups all-purpose flour**
> 1 **teaspoon ground ginger**
> ¾ **teaspoon baking soda**
> ¾ **teaspoon ground cinnamon**
> ½ **teaspoon ground cloves**
> ¼ **teaspoon salt**

1. In a blender, combine ice cream and cinnamon. Transfer to a freezer container; freeze for at least 2 hours.

2. Meanwhile, in a large bowl, cream the butter and brown sugar until light and fluffy. Add the egg, then molasses. Combine flour, ginger, baking soda, cinnamon, cloves and salt; gradually add to creamed mixture and mix well. Cover and refrigerate 2 hours or until easy to handle.

3. Preheat oven to 350°. On a lightly floured surface, roll dough to ⅛-in. thickness. Cut with a floured 3½-in. gingerbread-shaped cookie cutter. Place 1 in. apart on ungreased baking sheets. Bake 8-10 minutes or until edges are firm. Remove to wire racks to cool.

4. To make ice cream sandwiches, spread ¼ cup softened ice cream over the bottom of half of the cookies; top with remaining cookies. Wrap each in plastic wrap; freeze on a baking sheet at least 1 hour.

THE ELVIS ICE CREAM SANDWICH

PREP: 20 MIN. + FREEZING
MAKES: 4 SERVINGS

> ½ cup peanut butter chips
> 2 teaspoons shortening
> 2 cups peanut butter ice cream with peanut butter cup pieces, softened
> 8 slices banana bread
> 4 strips ready-to-serve fully cooked bacon, halved
> 1 tablespoon honey

1. In a microwave, melt peanut butter chips and shortening; stir until smooth. Cool slightly.

2. Spread peanut butter ice cream over half of the banana bread slices. Top with the bacon; drizzle with the melted peanut butter chips and honey. Top with the remaining banana bread. Wrap in plastic wrap; freeze on a baking sheet at least 1 hour.

> Celebrate the king of rock 'n' roll with a recipe inspired by some of Elvis' favorite foods—peanut butter, bananas and bacon.
>
> **—STEVEN SCHEND** GRAND RAPIDS, MI

CANDY BAR ICE CREAM SANDWICHES

Brownies, candy bar chunks and chocolate topping—what a combination! Everyone will love these irresistible treats.

—TASTE OF HOME TEST KITCHEN

PREP: 25 MIN. • **BAKE:** 10 MIN. + FREEZING
MAKES: 12-15 SERVINGS

> Brownie for Ice Cream Sandwiches (recipe on page 152)
> 4 cups Snickers ice cream, softened
> 1 bottle (7¼ ounces) chocolate hard-shell ice cream topping

1. Prepare, bake and cool the Brownie for Ice Cream Sandwiches according to the recipe directions.

2. Cut the cooled brownie in half widthwise. Spread the ice cream over one half of the brownie. Turn over the remaining brownie half; place over the ice cream. Cover and freeze for 2 hours or until firm.

3. Cut into bars, squares or desired shapes. Drizzle with the chocolate ice cream topping; let stand for 1-2 minutes or until chocolate topping is set. Wrap in plastic wrap; freeze on a baking sheet until serving.

HOMEMADE ICE CREAM SANDWICHES

What's better than made-from-scratch ice cream? It's so good sandwiched between cookies, whether they're fresh from your own oven or from the bakery.

—MEGUMI GARCIA MILWAUKEE, WI

PREP: 30 MIN. + FREEZING
MAKES: 9 SERVINGS

- 2 **tablespoons sugar**
- 1½ **teaspoons cornstarch**
- 1 **tablespoon butter, melted**
- ½ **cup 2% milk**
- ½ **teaspoon vanilla extract**
- ⅔ **cup sweetened condensed milk**
- 1 **cup heavy whipping cream**
- 1 **ounce semisweet chocolate, melted**
- 18 **chocolate chip or sugar cookies (3 inches)**
  Miniature semisweet chocolate chips, chocolate jimmies, chopped unsalted peanuts or flaked coconut, optional

1. In a small saucepan, combine sugar, cornstarch and butter; stir in the milk. Bring to a boil over medium heat; cook and stir 2 minutes or until thickened. Remove from heat; stir in vanilla. Cool completely. Stir in condensed milk.

2. In a large bowl, beat cream until stiff peaks form; fold into milk mixture. Divide between two freezer containers. Stir melted chocolate into one container until well blended. Cover and freeze both mixtures for 6 hours or until firm.

3. To make sandwiches, spread ⅓ cup of ice cream on bottoms of half of the cookies. Cover with remaining cookies; press down gently. If desired, roll sides of sandwiches in chips, jimmies, nuts or coconut. Wrap each in plastic wrap; freeze on a baking sheet until serving.

CHERRY-CHIP ICE CREAM SANDWICHES

One afternoon when I whipped up some cherry-chocolate chip ice cream, my kids came up with the idea of putting it between chocolate graham crackers. Yum!

—SALLY HOOK MONTGOMERY, TX

PREP: 15 MIN. + CHILLING
PROCESS: 20 MIN. + FREEZING
MAKES: 10 SERVINGS

1½ cups 2% milk
½ cup sugar
   Dash salt
 1 cup heavy whipping cream
 1 teaspoon vanilla extract
⅔ cup chopped dried cherries
½ cup miniature semisweet
   chocolate chips
10 whole chocolate graham crackers

1. In a large saucepan over medium heat, cook and stir milk, sugar and salt until sugar is dissolved. Remove from heat; stir in cream and vanilla. Transfer to a bowl; refrigerate until chilled.

2. Line a 13x9x2-in. pan with waxed paper; set aside. Fill the cylinder of ice cream freezer with milk mixture; freeze according to manufacturer's directions. Stir in the cherries and chocolate chips. Spread into prepared pan; cover and freeze overnight.

3. Cut or break the graham crackers in half. Using waxed paper, lift the ice cream out of pan; discard waxed paper. Cut the ice cream into squares the same size as the graham cracker halves; place the ice cream between cracker halves. Wrap sandwiches in plastic wrap; freeze on a baking sheet until serving.

AFTER-HOURS ICE CREAM SANDWICHES

Let the adults enjoy a fun coffee-flavored treat spiked with RumChata liqueur.

—SHAWN CARLETON SAN DIEGO, CA

PREP: 10 MIN. + FREEZING
MAKES: 4 SERVINGS

- 8 **teaspoons RumChata liqueur**
- 4 **ladyfingers, split**
- ½ **cup coffee ice cream, softened**
  Baking cocoa

1. Brush liqueur over the bottoms of the ladyfinger halves. Spread two tablespoons ice cream over the bottom of half of the ladyfingers. Top with remaining ladyfinger halves.

2. Wrap each in plastic wrap; freeze on a baking sheet at least 1 hour. Just before serving, dust with cocoa.

CANDY CRAZE ICE CREAM SANDWICHES

These frozen goodies have a little bit of everything to satisfy your sweet tooth.

—LAUREN KNOELKE MILWAUKEE, WI

PREP: 20 MIN. + FREEZING
MAKES: 4 SERVINGS

- 4 **scoops cookies and cream ice cream**
- 12 **large chocolate chip cookies**
- 4 **scoops peanut butter cup ice cream**
- ½ **cup M&M's minis, frozen**
- ½ **cup Reese's mini peanut butter cups**

1. Place a scoop of cookies and cream ice cream on each of four cookies. Top each with another cookie and a scoop of peanut butter cup ice cream. Top with remaining cookies.

2. Press the M&M's and peanut butter cups into the sides of sandwiches. Wrap in plastic wrap; freeze on a baking sheet at least 1 hour.

FROZEN SANDWICH COOKIES

With just three ingredients, these cute cookies are a snap to make. Everyone, young and old, snatches them up.

—MARY ANN IRVINE LOMBARD, IL

PREP: 10 MIN. + FREEZING
MAKES: 8 SANDWICH COOKIES

- ½ **cup spreadable strawberry cream cheese**
- ¼ **cup strawberry yogurt**
- 16 **chocolate wafers**

In a small bowl, beat cream cheese and yogurt until blended. Spread on bottoms of half of the chocolate wafers; top with remaining wafers. Place on a baking sheet. Freeze 30 minutes or until firm. Serve or wrap in plastic wrap and return to freezer for serving later.

IT'S-IT ICE CREAM SANDWICHES

Try the ice cream treat that's famous in San Francisco.
—JACYN SIEBERT SAN FRANCISCO, CA

PREP: 40 MIN. + FREEZING
BAKE: 15 MIN./BATCH + COOLING • **MAKES:** 7 SERVINGS

- ½ **cup butter, softened**
- ¾ **cup packed brown sugar**
- ¼ **cup sugar**
- 1 **egg**
- ½ **teaspoon vanilla extract**
- ¾ **cup all-purpose flour**
- ½ **teaspoon baking soda**
- ½ **teaspoon ground cinnamon**
- ¼ **teaspoon baking powder**
- ¼ **teaspoon salt**
- 1½ **cups quick-cooking oats**
- ¼ **cup chopped raisins, optional**

ASSEMBLY
- 3 **cups vanilla ice cream**
- 1 **bottle (7¼ ounces) chocolate hard-shell ice cream topping**

1. Preheat oven to 350°. In a large bowl, cream butter and sugars until light and fluffy. Beat in the egg and vanilla. In another bowl, whisk the flour, baking soda, cinnamon, baking powder and salt; gradually beat into creamed mixture. Stir in oats and, if desired, raisins.

2. Shape into fourteen 1¼-in. balls; place 2½ in. apart on ungreased baking sheets. Bake 11-13 minutes or until golden brown. Cool on pans 3 minutes. Remove to wire racks; cool completely.

3. To assemble sandwiches, place ⅓ cup ice cream on bottom of a cookie. Top with a second cookie, pressing gently to flatten ice cream. Place on a baking sheet; freeze until firm. Repeat with remaining cookies and ice cream.

4. Remove sandwiches from freezer. Working over a small bowl, drizzle chocolate topping over half of each sandwich, allowing excess to drip off.

5. Place on a waxed paper-lined baking sheet; freeze until serving. Wrap individually in plastic wrap for longer storage.

Oatmeal Cookie
Ice Cream Sandwiches

OATMEAL COOKIE ICE CREAM SANDWICHES

PREP: 35 MIN. • **BAKE:** 10 MIN. + FREEZING
MAKES: 10 SERVINGS

- ½ cup butter, softened
- ⅓ cup sugar
- ⅓ cup packed dark brown sugar
- 1 egg
- 2 teaspoons vanilla extract
- ⅔ cup all-purpose flour
- ½ teaspoon baking soda
- ¼ teaspoon salt
- ¼ teaspoon ground cinnamon
- 1½ cups quick-cooking oats
- ½ cup finely chopped semisweet chocolate
- 3 cups dulce de leche ice cream, softened if necessary
- ¼ cup brickle toffee bits

1. Preheat oven to 350°. In a large bowl, cream butter and sugars until light and fluffy. Beat in egg and vanilla. In another bowl, whisk flour, baking soda, salt and cinnamon; gradually beat into creamed mixture. Stir in oats and chocolate.

2. Shape cookie dough into twenty 1¼-in. balls. Place 2½ in. apart on ungreased baking sheets; flatten slightly with bottom of a glass dipped in sugar, smoothing the edges if necessary. Bake 10-13 minutes or until golden brown. Transfer from the pans to wire racks to cool completely.

3. Place ¼ cup ice cream on bottom of a cookie; sprinkle with 1 teaspoon toffee bits. Top with a second cookie, pressing gently to flatten ice cream. Place on a baking sheet; freeze overnight or until firm. Repeat with remaining cookies and ice cream. For longer storage, wrap the frozen sandwiches individually in plastic wrap and return to freezer.

These homemade oatmeal-chocolate chip cookies are to die for. Layer them with toffee bits and dulce de leche ice cream—you'll be in heaven! Sometimes I decorate the sides of the sandwiches with colorful jimmies, too.

—DIANE HALFERTY CORPUS CHRISTI, TX

CARAMEL-COFFEE ICE CREAM SANDWICHES

The java and dulce de leche flavors really perk up these frosty favorites. We coated the sides with chopped chocolate-covered coffee beans for good measure!
—*TASTE OF HOME* TEST KITCHEN

PREP: 25 MIN. • **BAKE:** 10 MIN. + FREEZING
MAKES: 12-15 SERVINGS

> **Brownie for Ice Cream Sandwiches (recipe at right)**
> 1 **teaspoon instant coffee granules**
> 4 **cups dulce de leche ice cream, softened**
> **Chocolate-covered coffee beans, chopped**

1. Prepare the batter for Brownie for Ice Cream Sandwiches; stir in the instant coffee granules. Bake and cool according to the recipe directions.
2. Cut the brownie in half widthwise. Spread the dulce de leche ice cream over one brownie half. Turn over the remaining brownie half; place over the ice cream. Cover; freeze for 2 hours or until firm.
3. Cut into bars, squares or desired shapes. Dip the sides of the ice cream sandwiches in chocolate-covered coffee beans. Wrap in plastic wrap; freeze on a baking sheet until serving.

BROWNIE FOR ICE CREAM SANDWICHES

This homemade brownie is perfect for creating ice cream sandwiches—simply add 4 cups of softened ice cream. Cut the brownie in half widthwise, spread one half with ice cream and top it with the other half. Wrap it in plastic wrap and freeze, then cut it into shapes. Want something a bit fancier? Try the treats listed at the end of this recipe.
—**LUCIE FITZGERALD** SPRING HILL, FL

PREP: 10 MIN. • **BAKE:** 10 MIN. + COOLING
MAKES: 12-15 SERVINGS

> ½ **cup butter, cubed**
> 4 **ounces semisweet chocolate, chopped**
> 2 **eggs**
> 1 **cup sugar**
> 1 **teaspoon vanilla extract**
> ¾ **cup all-purpose flour**
> ¼ **teaspoon salt**

1. Preheat oven to 400°. In microwave, melt butter and semisweet chocolate; stir until smooth. Cool slightly. In a large bowl, beat eggs and sugar. Stir in vanilla and chocolate mixture. Combine the flour and salt; gradually add to the chocolate mixture.
2. Pour the batter into a parchment paper-lined 15x10x1-in. baking pan. Bake 10-12 minutes or until center is set (do not overbake). Cool completely on a wire rack. Invert brownie onto a work surface and remove parchment paper.

BROWNIE FOR ICE CREAM SANDWICHES MAY BE USED TO PREPARE THE FOLLOWING RECIPES
Raspberry-Orange Ice Cream Sandwiches (p. 139), Candy Bar Ice Cream Sandwiches (p. 144) and Caramel-Coffee Ice Cream Sandwiches (at left).

ALL-STAR ICE CREAM SANDWICHES

Oreos and chunks of chocolate chip cookie dough will have family and friends cheering. You'll want to keep a supply in the freezer!

—SUSAN HEIN BURLINGTON, WI

PREP: 15 MIN. + FREEZING
MAKES: 4 SERVINGS

- ½ cup chocolate chip cookie dough ice cream, softened
- 8 Oreo cookies
- 6 ounces milk chocolate candy coating, melted
  Red, white and blue sprinkles

Spoon 2 tablespoons chocolate chip cookie dough ice cream onto half of the cookies. Top with remaining cookies. Spoon the melted milk chocolate candy coating over the tops. Decorate with sprinkles. Freeze on a baking sheet at least 1 hour.

COATING CLUE

Candy coating is sometimes called dipping chocolate or confectionery coating. It's sold in many different forms. At your store, you may find it in large individual blocks, packages of flat disks or chips, or boxes of individually wrapped 1-ounce squares.

ICY
POPS

STRAWBERRY-ROSEMARY YOGURT POPS

PREP: 20 MIN. + FREEZING • **MAKES:** 6 POPS

- 1 **cup chopped fresh strawberries**
- 2 **tablespoons balsamic vinegar**
- 2 **tablespoons strawberry preserves**
- 2 **fresh rosemary sprigs**
- 1½ **cups (12 ounces) vanilla yogurt**
- 6 **freezer pop molds or paper cups (3 ounces each) and wooden pop or lollipop sticks**

1. In a small bowl, mix strawberries, vinegar, preserves and rosemary. Let stand 30 minutes; discard rosemary.

2. Spoon 2 tablespoons yogurt and 1 tablespoon strawberry mixture into each mold or paper cup. Repeat layers. Top molds with holders. If using cups, top with foil and insert sticks through foil. Freeze until firm.

We planted strawberries a few years ago, and these tangy-sweet frozen yogurt pops are my very favorite treat to make with them! The options are endless. Try using other yogurt flavors, like lemon, raspberry or blueberry. You may also substitute one of your favorite herbs for the rosemary or simply omit it.
—**CARMELL CHILDS** FERRON, UT

STRAWBERRY MALLOW POPS

Everyone in my family enjoys these strawberry pops, especially on hot days. I try to keep a cache in the freezer. The bits of fruit and marshmallow make them especially fun to eat.

—ARLENE PICKARD REDVERS, SK

PREP: 20 MIN. + FREEZING
MAKES: 2 DOZEN

- 1 **package (8 ounces) cream cheese, softened**
- ¼ **cup honey**
- 2 **packages (10 ounces each) frozen sweetened sliced strawberries, thawed**
- 3 **cups miniature marshmallows**
- 1 **cup heavy whipping cream, whipped**
- 24 **freezer pop molds or 24 paper cups (3 ounces each) and wooden pop sticks**

1. In a small bowl, beat cream cheese and honey until smooth. Add the strawberries with juice; beat until blended. Fold in marshmallows and whipped cream.

2. Pour ¼ cupfuls into molds or cups. Top molds with holders. If using cups, top with foil and insert sticks through foil. Freeze until firm.

ICY FRUIT POPS

My grandmother made these treats for my brother and me when we were little. I've lightened them up a bit, and they remain a cool and simple snack that always delights.
—**LEANN KANE** FORSYTH, IL

PREP: 20 MIN. + FREEZING
MAKES: 2 DOZEN

- 1 **can (20 ounces) crushed pineapple, undrained**
- 1 **cup water**
- ¾ **cup thawed orange juice concentrate**
- ¾ **cup thawed lemonade concentrate**
  Sugar substitute equivalent to ½ cup sugar
- 5 **medium firm bananas, cut into ¼-inch slices and quartered**
- 1 **can (12 ounces) diet ginger ale**
- 24 **maraschino cherries or fresh strawberries**
- 24 **freezer pop molds or 24 paper cups (3 ounces each) and wooden pop sticks**

1. In a large bowl, combine pineapple, water, orange juice concentrate, lemonade concentrate and sugar substitute. Stir in the bananas and ginger ale.

2. Place a cherry in each mold or cup; fill with pineapple mixture. Top molds with holders. If using cups, top with foil and insert sticks through foil. Freeze until firm.

NOTE *This recipe was tested with Splenda no-calorie sweetener.*

Cool Watermelon Pops

COOL WATERMELON POPS

PREP: 20 MIN. + FREEZING • **MAKES:** 28 POPS

- 2 **cups boiling water**
- 1 **cup sugar**
- 1 **package (3 ounces) watermelon gelatin**
- 1 **envelope unsweetened watermelon cherry Kool-Aid mix**
- 2 **cups refrigerated watermelon juice blend**
- ⅓ **cup miniature semisweet chocolate chips**
- 2 **cups prepared limeade**
- 2 **to 3 teaspoons green food coloring, optional**
- 28 **freezer pop molds or 28 paper cups (3 ounces each) and wooden pop sticks**

1. In a large bowl, combine the water, sugar, gelatin and Kool-Aid mix; stir until sugar is dissolved. Add watermelon juice. Fill each mold or cup with 3 tablespoons watermelon mixture. Freeze until almost slushy, about 1 hour. Sprinkle with chocolate chips. Top molds with holders. If using cups, top with foil and insert sticks through foil. Freeze.

2. In a small bowl, combine limeade and food coloring if desired. If using freezer molds, remove holders. If using paper cups, remove foil. Pour limeade mixture over tops. Return holders or foil. Freeze until firm.

The kids are going to flip for the miniature chocolate chips in these picture-perfect pops. They're almost too cute to eat (but you'll be glad you did).
—*TASTE OF HOME* TEST KITCHEN

HOMEMADE FUDGE POPS

On hot summer days, these are my kids' favorite frozen treats. I like knowing exactly what's in these pops, and they're not very expensive to make!

—LYSSA PRASEK VITA, MB

PREP: 30 MIN. + FREEZING
MAKES: 20 SERVINGS

- ¼ **cup butter, cubed**
- ½ **cup all-purpose flour**
- 4 **cups milk**
- 1⅓ **cups packed brown sugar**
- ⅓ **cup baking cocoa**
- 1 **teaspoon salt**
- 2 **teaspoons vanilla extract**
- 20 **freezer pop molds or 20 paper cups (3 ounces each) and wooden pop sticks**

1. In a large saucepan, melt butter over medium heat. Stir in flour until smooth; gradually add milk. Stir in the brown sugar, cocoa and salt. Bring to a boil; cook and stir for 2 minutes or until thickened.

2. Remove from the heat; stir in vanilla. Cool mixture for 20 minutes, stirring several times.

3. Pour ¼ cup mixture into molds or paper cups. Top molds with holders. If using cups, top with foil and insert sticks through foil. Freeze until firm.

BERRY BLUE POPS

You'll have a blast swirling together the colorful mixes in these berrylicious pops.

—TASTE OF HOME TEST KITCHEN

PREP: 25 MIN. + FREEZING
MAKES: 18 POPS

- 6 **tablespoons berry blue gelatin**
- 1 **cup sugar, divided**
- 2 **cups boiling water, divided**
- 2 **cups cold water, divided**
- 6 **tablespoons strawberry gelatin**
- 18 **freezer pop molds or 18 paper cups (3 ounces each) and wooden pop sticks**

1. Dissolve berry gelatin and ½ cup sugar in 1 cup boiling water. Stir in 1 cup cold water. In another bowl, repeat procedure with strawberry gelatin, remaining sugar and remaining waters.

2. Combine half of berry mixture and half of strawberry mixture in a small bowl. Freeze all three mixtures for 1¾ to 2 hours or until slushy. In a large bowl, swirl the three colors as desired. Fill each mold or cup with ¼ cup of the gelatin mixture. Top with holders. If using cups, top with foil and insert sticks through foil. Freeze until firm.

BOURBON VANILLA

Most vanilla comes from Madagascar and Reunion Island—formerly known as the Bourbon Islands—off the southeast coast of Africa. Bourbon vanilla has a strong, clear vanilla flavor and creamy finish.

ORANGE ICE CREAM POPS

Orange juice and vanilla ice cream prove to be ideal partners in these tasty pops.

—ANTOINETTE RONZIO

NORTH PROVIDENCE, RI

PREP: 10 MIN. + FREEZING
MAKES: 1 DOZEN

- 1 **cup cold milk**
- 2 **cups vanilla ice cream**
- 1 **can (6 ounces) frozen orange juice concentrate, partially thawed**

12 **freezer pop molds or 12 paper cups (3 ounces each) and wooden pop sticks**

1. In a blender, combine the millk, ice cream and orange juice concentrate; cover and process until smooth.

2. Pour ¼ cupfuls into molds or cups. Top molds with holders. If using cups, top with foil and insert sticks through foil. Freeze until firm.

Frozen Fruit
Yogurt Pops

FROZEN FRUIT YOGURT POPS

PREP: 15 MIN. + FREEZING
MAKES: 1 DOZEN

- 2¼ **cups (18 ounces) raspberry yogurt**
- 2 **tablespoons lemon juice**
- 2 **medium ripe bananas, cut into chunks**
- 12 **freezer pop molds or 12 paper cups (3 ounces each) and wooden pop sticks**

1. Place the yogurt, lemon juice and bananas in a blender; cover and process until smooth, stopping to stir mixture if necessary.
2. Pour mixture into molds or paper cups. Top molds with holders. If using cups, top with foil and insert sticks through foil. Freeze until firm.

> My grandson, Patrick, who's now in high school, was "Grammy's helper" for years. We made these frozen pops for company and everyone, including the adults, loved them. They're delicious and good for you!
> —**JUNE DICKENSON** PHILIPPI, WV

BLACKBERRY MINT POPS

Classic pops get a gourmet makeover when blackberries and mint collide.
—**MYRNA CAMPBELL** PHILOMATH, OR

PREP: 20 MIN. + FREEZING
MAKES: 16 POPS

- 2 **cups water**
- 1 **cup packed brown sugar**
- 2 **cups strained blackberry puree (from 4 cups fresh blackberries)**
- ¼ **cup minced fresh mint**
- 16 **freezer pop molds or 16 paper cups (3 ounces each) and wooden pop sticks**

1. In a small saucepan, bring water and brown sugar to a boil. Cook and stir until sugar is dissolved. Stir in blackberry puree and mint.
2. Fill molds or cups with ¼ cup fruit mixture. Freeze for 1 hour or until slushy. Gently stir to distribute mint. Top molds with holders. If using cups, top with foil and insert sticks through foil. Freeze until firm.

BLUEBERRY FIZZ POPS

The whole family will go bananas when they taste my fizzy concoction of frozen berries and grape juice. Let's see those smiling purple lips.

—**MARGIE HAEN** MENOMONEE FALLS, WI

PREP: 20 MIN. + FREEZING
MAKES: 16 POPS

- 2 **cups fresh or frozen blueberries**
- 1 **medium ripe banana**
- 3 **to 4 drops neon purple food coloring, optional**
- 2 **cups sparkling Concord grape juice**
- 16 **freezer pop molds or 16 paper cups (3 ounces each) and wooden pop sticks**

1. Place blueberries, banana and, if desired, food coloring in a blender; cover and process until smooth. Add grape juice and process until blended.
2. Fill each mold or cup with ¼ cup of the blueberry mixture. Top molds with holders. If using cups, top with foil and insert sticks through foil. Freeze until firm.

STRAWBERRY-MANGO DAIQUIRI POPS

When hosting a summer party for adults, offer them these irresistible treats. They have a kiss of tropical flavor.

—*TASTE OF HOME* TEST KITCHEN

PREP: 20 MIN. + FREEZING
MAKES: 20 POPS

- 1 **cup water**
- ½ **cup mango nectar**
- ¼ **cup light rum**
- 3 **tablespoons lime juice**
- 1 **pound halved fresh strawberries**
- 1 **cup coarsely chopped peeled mango**

- ⅓ **cup sugar**
- 20 **freezer pop molds or 20 paper cups (3 ounces each) and wooden pop sticks**

1. Place half of the water, mango nectar, rum, lime juice, strawberries, mango and sugar in a blender; cover and process until blended.
2. Pour ¼ cup mixture into each of 10 molds or paper cups; top molds with holders. If using cups, top with foil and insert sticks through foil. Repeat with the remaining ingredients and molds. Freeze until firm.

FUDGY ALMOND POPS

Amaretto creamer is the surprise ingredient that enhances the almond flavor of these fudge pops.

—**SHARON GUINTA** STAMFORD, CT

PREP: 10 MIN. + FREEZING
MAKES: 8 POPS

- 2 **cups whole milk**
- 1 **package (3.9 ounces) instant chocolate fudge pudding mix**
- ½ **cup sugar**
- ½ **cup amaretto-flavored refrigerated nondairy creamer**
- ⅛ **teaspoon almond extract**
- 8 **freezer pop molds or 8 paper cups (3 ounces each) and wooden pop sticks**

In a large bowl, whisk the milk, pudding mix, sugar, creamer and extract for 2 minutes or until creamy. Pour into molds or cups. Top molds with holders. If using cups, top with foil and insert sticks through foil. Freeze until firm.

FRUIT JUICE POPS

I've used this recipe for years. My children enjoyed these refreshing treats more than any of the store-bought ones I ever brought home. They taste great made with either pineapple or orange juice. Try freezing them and serving in "cups" made from hollowed-out oranges.

—BARBARA STEWART GARLAND, TX

PREP: 25 MIN. + FREEZING
MAKES: 1 DOZEN

- 2 **cups water**
- 1½ **cups sugar**
- 4 **cups unsweetened apple juice**
- 1 **cup unsweetened pineapple or orange juice**
- ½ **cup lemon juice**
- 12 **freezer pop molds or 12 paper cups (3 ounces each) and wooden pop sticks**

1. In a large saucepan, combine water and sugar; bring to a boil. Reduce heat; simmer, uncovered, for 3-4 minutes or until sugar is dissolved, stirring occasionally. Remove from the heat; stir in juices.

2. Fill molds or cups with ¼ cup juice mixture. Top molds with holders. If using cups, top with foil and insert sticks through foil. Freeze until firm.

MAPLE MOCHA POPS

My husband says one of these creamy pops is just not enough. They're a breeze to make, and kids love them, too. For a more grownup presentation, freeze them in pretty serving cups and add a dollop of whipped cream.

—**CAROLINE SPERRY** ALLENTOWN, MI

PREP: 15 MIN. + FREEZING
MAKES: 1 DOZEN

- **2   cups heavy whipping cream**
- **½   cup half-and-half cream**
- **¼   cup maple syrup**
- **¼   cup chocolate syrup**
- **1   tablespoon instant coffee granules**
- **12   freezer pop molds or 12 paper cups (3 ounces each) and wooden pop sticks**

1. In a large bowl, whisk whipping cream, half-and-half, maple syrup, chocolate syrup and coffee granules until coffee is dissolved.

2. Fill molds or cups with ¼ cup cream mixture. Top molds with holders. If using cups, top with foil and insert sticks through foil. Freeze until firm.

LEMON-APRICOT FRUIT POPS

With just 31 calories, a dash of sugar and lots of vitamin C, this is one light, refreshing summer dessert everyone can find room for!

—AYSHA SCHURMAN AMMON, ID

PREP: 15 MIN. + FREEZING
MAKES: 6 SERVINGS

- **1 cup sliced fresh apricots**
- **½ cup ice cubes**
- **¼ cup lemon juice**
- **¼ cup orange juice**
- **4 teaspoons sugar**
- **1 teaspoon grated lemon peel**
- **1 teaspoon minced fresh mint, optional**
- **6 freezer pop molds or 6 paper cups (3 ounces each) and wooden pop sticks**

In a blender, combine first six ingredients; stir in mint if desired. Fill each mold or cup with ¼ cup apricot mixture. Top molds with holders. If using cups, top with foil and insert sticks through the foil. Freeze until firm.

TROPICAL STRAWBERRY POPS

Banana and pineapple bring a taste of the tropics to these icy treats bursting with sweet strawberry flavor. What's not to love?

—TASTE OF HOME TEST KITCHEN

PREP: 10 MIN. + FREEZING
MAKES: 1½ DOZEN

- **2 cups strawberry-banana V8 juice blend**
- **1 can (8 ounces) unsweetened crushed pineapple, undrained**
- **1 cup frozen unsweetened strawberries, thawed**
- **1 medium banana**
- **18 freezer pop molds or 18 paper cups (3 ounces each) and wooden pop sticks**

Place juice, pineapple, strawberries and banana in a blender; cover and process until pureed. Fill each mold or cup with ¼ cup strawberry mixture. Top molds with holders. If using cups, top with foil and insert sticks through foil. Freeze until firm.

FROZEN YOGURT

Here's a super-easy idea: Push a wooden pop stick through the foil cover of a small yogurt. (Remove any plastic lid first.) Then just freeze, remove the plastic container and enjoy!

CHOCOLATE HAZELNUT SOY POPS

PREP: 10 MIN. + FREEZING
MAKES: 8 POPS

- 1 **cup vanilla soy milk**
- ½ **cup fat-free milk**
- ¾ **cup fat-free vanilla Greek yogurt**
- ⅓ **cup Nutella**
- 8 **freezer pop molds or 8 paper cups (3 ounces each) and wooden pop sticks**

Place milks, yogurt and Nutella in a blender; cover and process until smooth. Pour into molds or paper cups. Top molds with holders, If using cups, top with foil and insert sticks through foil. Freeze until firm.

> I love Nutella, and I'm always looking for ways to use it. These pops are a great way to stay cool in the summer, but also make a cozy treat in the winter.
>
> —**BONITA SUTER** LAWRENCE, MI

Chocolate Hazelnut
Soy Pops

COCONUT PINEAPPLE POPS

You'll love the pairing of pineapple and coconut in these sensational treats. With their sunny color and creamy texture, these pretty pops just might be your hottest fresh-from-the-freezer treat!

—*TASTE OF HOME* TEST KITCHEN

PREP: 10 MIN. + FREEZING
MAKES: 14 POPS

- 1½ **cups cold 2% milk**
- 1 **can (8 ounces) unsweetened crushed pineapple**
- 1 **can (6 ounces) unsweetened pineapple juice**
- 1 **teaspoon coconut extract**
- 1 **package (3.4 ounces) instant vanilla pudding mix**
- 14 **freezer pop molds or 14 paper cups (3 ounces each) and wooden pop sticks**

1. In a blender, combine the milk, pineapple, pineapple juice and extract; cover and process until smooth. Pour into a bowl; whisk in pudding mix for 2 minutes.

2. Pour ¼ cup into each mold or paper cups. Top the molds with holders. If using cups, top with foil and insert sticks through foil. Freeze until firm.

WHITE BERRY ICE POPS

I think it's safe to say you'll love these ice pops speckled with colorful mixed berries.
—**SHARON GUINTA** STAMFORD, CT

PREP: 10 MIN. + FREEZING
MAKES: 10 POPS

- 1¾ **cups whole milk**
- 1 **tablespoon honey**
- ¼ **teaspoon vanilla extract**
- 1 **package (12 ounces) frozen unsweetened mixed berries, thawed and drained**
- 10 **freezer pop molds or 10 paper cups (3 ounces each) and wooden pop sticks**

In a small bowl, whisk the milk, honey and vanilla. Evenly divide the berries among molds or cups. Pour the milk mixture over berries. Top molds with holders. If using cups, top with foil and insert sticks through foil. Freeze until firm.

CRAZY-COLORED FRUIT POPS

Orange, pear, banana, raspberry, grape—the gang's all here! See if your poolside pals can guess all the flavors in one of these summery rainbow pops.
—**VIKKI SPENGLER** OCALA, FL

PREP: 20 MIN. + FREEZING
MAKES: 19 POPS

- 1 **cup orange-tangerine juice**
- 2 **cans (15 ounces each) reduced-sugar sliced pears, drained, divided**
- 1 **medium banana, sliced, divided**
- 2 **to 3 drops yellow food coloring, optional**
- 4 **drops red food coloring, optional, divided**
- 1 **cup red raspberry juice**
- 1 **cup grape juice**
- 19 **freezer pop molds or 19 paper cups (3 ounces each) and wooden pop sticks**

1. In a blender, combine orange-tangerine juice, ¾ cup pears, a third of the banana slices, yellow food coloring and, if desired, 1 drop red food coloring; cover and process until smooth. Fill each mold or cup with 1 tablespoon mixture. Top molds with holders. If using cups, top with foil and insert sticks through foil. Freeze 30 minutes or until firm.

2. In a blender, combine raspberry juice, ¾ cup pears, a third of the banana slices and, if desired, red food coloring; cover and process until smooth. If using pop molds, remove holders. If using cups, remove foil. Pour raspberry mixture over orange layer. Return holders or foil. Freeze 30 minutes or until firm.

3. In a blender, combine grape juice, remaining pears and remaining banana slices; cover and process until smooth. If using pop molds, remove holders. If using cups, remove foil. Pour grape mixture over tops; return holders or foil. Freeze 30 minutes or until firm.

QUICK BANANA POP

Cut a banana in half, insert a wooden pop stick and freeze. Dip the pop in maple syrup, honey or melted chocolate, then roll in chopped nuts or cookie crumbs and return to the freezer.

SUPER
SUNDAES

ORANGE DREAM PARFAITS

PREP: 15 MIN. + FREEZING • **MAKES:** 6 SERVINGS

- 4 **ounces cream cheese, softened**
- 4½ **teaspoons sugar**
- ¾ **teaspoon vanilla extract**
- ¾ **cup miniature marshmallows**
- 1½ **cups heavy whipping cream, whipped, divided**
- 3 **cups orange sherbet, softened**
- 6 **clear plastic cups (8 ounces each)**

1. In a small bowl, beat cream cheese, sugar and vanilla until smooth; fold in the miniature marshmallows and half of the whipped cream. Set aside. In another bowl, fold the remaining whipped cream into orange sherbet.

2. Spoon ¼ cup orange sherbet mixture into each clear plastic cup; top with 3 tablespoons cream cheese mixture. Repeat the layers. Cover and freeze for 3 hours or until firm. Remove from the freezer 15 minutes before serving.

These cool cups blend the classic flavors of orange and vanilla with the richness of cream cheese. They're great to make ahead for a party.
—*TASTE OF HOME* TEST KITCHEN

COFFEE ICE CREAM COOKIE CUPS

Since I was a child, I've loved trying out new recipes. I came up with cookie cups for my sister's birthday. This version is my favorite, but feel free to substitute peanut butter dough or a different ice cream flavor.

—MARCUS DOOLEY RED OAK, TX

PREP: 30 MIN. • **BAKE:** 15 MIN. + FREEZING
MAKES: 12 SERVINGS

- **1 tube (16½ ounces) refrigerated chocolate chip cookie dough**
- **2 cups coffee ice cream**
  Whipped cream and chocolate syrup
- **⅓ cup English toffee bits or almond brickle chips**

1. Preheat oven to 350°. Let the chocolate chip cookie dough stand at room temperature 5-10 minutes to soften. Cut into 12 slices; press onto the bottoms and up the sides of greased muffin cups.

2. Bake 12-14 minutes or until golden brown. Cool slightly on a wire rack. Spoon coffee ice cream into each cup. Cover; freeze 1-2 hours or until firm.

3. Remove cups from pan. Garnish with whipped cream and chocolate syrup. Sprinkle with toffee bits.

BANANA RUM SUNDAES

Here's an easy dessert for a busy weeknight. The recipe takes just 20 minutes to prepare from start to finish, and everyone enjoys the warm topping full of glazed bananas. You could also serve it over slices of cake.

—DENISE ALBERS FREEBURG, IL

START TO FINISH: 20 MIN.
MAKES: 6 SERVINGS

- 3 **tablespoons butter**
- ¾ **cup packed brown sugar**
  Dash ground nutmeg
- 4 **medium firm bananas, halved and sliced**
- ¼ **cup golden raisins**
- ¼ **cup rum**
- 2 **tablespoons sliced almonds, toasted**
- 1 **quart vanilla ice cream**

1. In a large nonstick skillet, melt the butter over medium-low heat. Stir in brown sugar and nutmeg until blended.
2. Remove from heat; add the bananas, golden raisins, rum and almonds. Cook over medium heat, stirring gently, for 3-4 minutes or until the bananas are glazed and slightly softened. Serve with vanilla ice cream.

Mexican
Ice Cream Sundaes

MEXICAN ICE CREAM SUNDAES

Whether you're throwing a Cinco de Mayo party or just having a south-of-the-border dinner, these sundaes make the perfect sweet treat. The cinnamon-spiced fried tortilla wedges add a crunchy accent.

—MILBERT FICHTER PITTSBURGH, PA

PREP: 30 MIN. + FREEZING
MAKES: 6 SERVINGS

- ½ **cup canola oil**
- 6 **flour tortillas (6 inches), cut into 6 wedges each**
- 2 **tablespoons sugar**
- ½ **teaspoon ground cinnamon**
- ¼ **cup crushed cornflakes**
- 6 **large scoops vanilla ice cream**
  Chocolate syrup, optional
  Whipped cream in a can
- 6 **maraschino cherries with stems**

1. In a large skillet, heat canola oil over medium heat. Fry tortilla wedges, a few at a time, for 1-2 minutes on each side or until crisp. Drain on paper towels. Combine the sugar and cinnamon; set aside 1 tablespoon. Sprinkle both sides of tortilla wedges with the remaining cinnamon sugar.
2. In a shallow bowl, combine crushed cornflakes and reserved cinnamon sugar. Roll scoops of ice cream in crumb mixture to coat. Freeze until serving.
3. Drizzle serving plates with chocolate syrup if desired. Place six tortilla wedges on each plate; top each with a scoop of ice cream. Pipe whipped cream around the base and on top of ice cream. Garnish each with a maraschino cherry.

ICE CREAM TORTILLA CUPS

These little cups are so easy to create using flour tortillas. Just brush them with butter, sprinkle on cinnamon sugar, press them into a muffin tin and bake.

—KELLY OLSON MOAB, UT

START TO FINISH: 25 MIN.
MAKES: 6 SERVINGS

- ¼ **cup butter, melted**
- 6 **flour tortillas (6 inches), warmed**
- 6 **tablespoons sugar**
- ½ **teaspoon ground cinnamon**
    Strawberry ice cream or flavor of your choice

1. Preheat oven to 400°. Brush butter on one side of each tortilla. Combine sugar and cinnamon; sprinkle evenly over tortillas. Press each tortilla, sugar side up, into a greased muffin cup.
2. Bake 6-8 minutes or until lightly browned. Cool 5 minutes. Gently separate the edges. Place a scoop of ice cream in each tortilla.

CHOCOLATE MARSHMALLOW SUNDAES

I've been making chocolate sundaes with marshmallow creme for decades, and I've yet to find a commercial version that equals them in velvety texture and taste.

—LILY JULOW LAWRENCEVILLE, GA

PREP: 20 MIN. + FREEZING
MAKES: 12 SERVINGS

- 2 **cups heavy whipping cream**
- ⅔ **cup sweetened condensed milk**
- ⅔ **cup chocolate syrup**
- ½ **teaspoon vanilla extract**
SUNDAES
- 1½ **cups marshmallow creme**
- ½ **cup chocolate syrup**
- ⅔ **cup whipped cream**
- ¼ **cup chopped almonds, toasted**
- 12 **maraschino cherries**

1. In a large bowl, beat cream, milk, chocolate syrup and vanilla until soft peaks form. Transfer to a 9-in.-square pan. Cover; freeze for at least 4 hours.
2. In each of 12 dessert dishes, place 3 tablespoons frozen mixture and 1 tablespoon marshmallow creme; repeat the layers. Top each with 2 teaspoons syrup, scant tablespoon whipped cream, 1 teaspoon almonds and a cherry. Serve immediately.

BANANA SPLIT COOKIE TRIFLES

Layered with cookie bits and traditional banana split toppings, these personal-size trifles delight kids and adults alike.

—MARCI CARL NORTHERN CAMBRIA, PA

START TO FINISH: 15 MIN.
MAKES: 4 SERVINGS

- 4 **soft chocolate chip cookies, crumbled**
- 2 **cups chocolate chip ice cream, softened**
- 2 **small bananas, halved lengthwise and cut into 1-inch pieces**
- ½ **cup whipped cream**
- ⅔ **cup hot fudge ice cream topping**

Place 1 tablespoon cookie crumbs in each of four dessert dishes. Layer with half of the chocolate chip ice cream, bananas, whipped cream, fudge topping and remaining cookies. Repeat layers. Serve immediately.

FROSTY MUD PIES

After seeing recipes that use prepared graham cracker pie crusts and ice cream, I started experimenting in the kitchen and came up with my own combination based on the classic Mississippi mud pie. I love that I can whip these up without any baking.

—CASSANDRA GOURLEY WILLIAMS, AZ

START TO FINISH: 10 MIN.
MAKES: 4 SERVINGS

⅔ cup Nutella
4 **individual graham cracker tart shells**
1 **pint coffee ice cream**
   Whipped cream and chocolate-covered coffee beans

Spoon Nutella into graham cracker tart shells. Top each with coffee ice cream; garnish with the whipped cream and chocolate-covered coffee beans.

CANDY BAR PARFAITS

Kids love making their own frosty treats. These are such a favorite, I've served them at build-your-own-parfait birthday parties. For even more fun, offer a variety of nuts, candy bars and ice cream flavors.
—**ANGIE CASSADA** MONROE, NC

START TO FINISH: 10 MIN.
MAKES: 4 SERVINGS

- ½ **cup coarsely chopped unsalted peanuts**
- ½ **cup coarsely crushed pretzels**
- 1 **milk chocolate candy bar (1.55 ounces), chopped**
- 1 **pint vanilla ice cream, softened**
- ⅓ **cup chocolate syrup**
- 2 **tablespoons peanut butter**

1. In a small bowl, combine the chopped peanuts, crushed pretzels and chopped milk chocolate candy bar; spoon 2 tablespoons into each of four parfait glasses. Top each with ¼ cup vanilla ice cream, 2 tablespoons peanut mixture and another ¼ cup ice cream.
2. Combine chocolate syrup and peanut butter; drizzle over the ice cream. Sprinkle with the remaining peanut mixture.

PRALINE-PEACH BROWNIE SUNDAES

START TO FINISH: 20 MIN.
MAKES: 6 SERVINGS

- ¼ cup packed brown sugar
- ¼ cup heavy whipping cream
- 2 tablespoons butter
- ¼ teaspoon ground cinnamon
- 2 medium peaches, peeled and sliced, or 1 cup frozen unsweetened peach slices, thawed and patted dry
- ½ cup chopped pecans
- 1 teaspoon vanilla extract
- 6 prepared brownies
- 3 cups vanilla ice cream
  Additional peach slices, optional

1. In a large saucepan, whisk brown sugar, heavy whipping cream, butter and cinnamon until smooth. Bring to a boil; cook and stir for 6-7 minutes or until thickened. Remove from the heat; stir in the peaches, pecans and vanilla. Cool for 10 minutes.

2. Place brownies in dessert dishes; top with ice cream and peach sauce. Garnish with additional peach slices if desired.

> Adding fresh sliced peaches to a homemade praline sauce creates an irresistible topping. It really dresses up sundaes made with store-bought brownies.
> —**JODI TRIGG** TOLEDO, IL

CHERRY CAPPUCCINO SUNDAES

I adapted a newspaper recipe and came up with these yummy desserts. A sprinkling of grated chocolate is the finishing touch.
—**J. A. ROGG** PHILADELPHIA, PA

START TO FINISH: 15 MIN.
MAKES: 2 SERVINGS

- ½ cup milk
- ¾ cup pitted dark sweet cherries
- ½ teaspoon honey
- ¼ teaspoon almond extract
  Coffee or cappuccino ice cream
- 2 tablespoons grated semisweet chocolate, optional

In a blender, combine the first four ingredients; cover and process until blended. Serve over ice cream. Sprinkle with grated chocolate if desired.

PUMPKIN PECAN SUNDAES

My family enjoys anything with pumpkin, so I knew this recipe would be a winner. Butter pecan ice cream is a wonderful complement to the spiced sauce.

—FANCHEON RESLER ALBION, IN

START TO FINISH: 20 MIN.
MAKES: 6 SERVINGS

- ⅓ **cup sugar**
- 2 **teaspoons cornstarch**
- ¼ **teaspoon each ground ginger, cinnamon and nutmeg**
- 1 **cup canned pumpkin**
- ⅔ **cup 2% milk**
- 1½ **teaspoons vanilla extract, divided**
- 1 **cup heavy whipping cream**
- 3 **tablespoons confectioners' sugar**
- 3 **cups butter pecan ice cream**
- 6 **tablespoons chopped pecans, toasted**

1. In a small saucepan, combine the sugar, cornstarch and spices. Stir in the pumpkin and milk until smooth. Bring to a boil; cook and stir for 2 minutes or until thickened. Remove from the heat; stir in 1 teaspoon vanilla.

2. In a small bowl, beat heavy whipping cream until it begins to thicken. Add the confectioners' sugar and remaining vanilla; beat until stiff peaks form.

3. Scoop butter pecan ice cream into six dessert dishes. Top each with ¼ cup pumpkin sauce and ⅓ cup whipped cream. Sprinkle with pecans.

BEATING CREAM

To determine whether heavy whipping cream has reached the "stiff peaks" stage during beating, lift up the beaters. The peaks of the cream should stand straight up, not curl over. Also, if you tilt the mixing bowl, the cream should not slide around.

Pumpkin
Pecan Sundaes

STRAWBERRY SUNDAE CUPS

I received this three-ingredient sundae recipe years ago, and it's definitely a keeper. The homemade chocolate cups are a snap to make. For an extra-special touch, garnish them with chocolate hearts.

—SANDRA NATERA TUCSON, AZ

PREP: 15 MIN. + FREEZING
MAKES: 2 SERVINGS

- **4 ounces bittersweet chocolate, chopped**
- **2 scoops strawberry ice cream**
  Whipped cream in a can

1. In a microwave, melt 3 ounces of chocolate; stir until smooth. Brush chocolate evenly on inside of two foil muffin cup liners. Freeze for 10 minutes or until set. Repeat the brushing and freezing steps two more times.

2. Melt remaining chocolate; transfer to a small resealable plastic bag. Cut a small hole in a corner of the bag. Pipe two heart shapes onto waxed paper. Freeze until set.

3. Just before serving, carefully peel liners off of chocolate cups and discard. Fill with ice cream. Garnish with the whipped cream and chocolate hearts.

CARAMEL YOGURT SUNDAES

Warm caramel sauce served over vanilla frozen yogurt? It's spoon-licking good on a summer evening or anytime.

—MARLENE KROLL CHICAGO, IL

START TO FINISH: 15 MIN.
MAKES: 1½ CUPS

- ½ **cup butter, cubed**
- 1 **cup packed brown sugar**
- ½ **cup heavy whipping cream**
- 3 **teaspoons vanilla extract**
  Low-fat vanilla frozen yogurt

1. In a small saucepan, heat the butter over medium heat. Add brown sugar; cook and stir for 3-4 minutes or until sugar is dissolved.

2. Add heavy whipping cream; bring to a boil, stirring constantly. Remove from the heat; stir in vanilla. Serve warm over frozen yogurt. Cover and refrigerate any leftover sauce.

TRICKY TACO CUPS

People of all ages fall in love with these sneaky sweets that resemble taco salads. The crunchy waffle bowls are filled with ice cream, then topped with tinted coconut for the lettuce and cheese, halved maraschino cherries for the tomatoes and black rope licorice for the ripe olives. Fun!

—TASTE OF HOME TEST KITCHEN

PREP: 20 MIN. + FREEZING
MAKES: 6 SERVINGS

- 1 **cup ground pecans**
- 1 **pint chocolate or vanilla ice cream**
- 1¾ **teaspoons water, divided**
- 6 **drops green food coloring**
- 1¾ **cups flaked coconut, divided**
- 4 **drops yellow food coloring**
- 6 **waffle ice cream bowls**
- 6 **tablespoons whipped topping**
- 3 **pieces black rope licorice, cut into ¼-inch slices**
- 9 **maraschino cherries, patted dry, halved**

1. Place the pecans in a shallow bowl. Drop small scoops of ice cream into pecans; roll to coat. Place on a baking sheet; freeze until firm.

2. In a large resealable plastic bag, combine 1½ teaspoons water and green food coloring; add 1½ cups coconut. Seal the bag and shake to tint. In a small resealable plastic bag, combine yellow food coloring and remaining water; add remaining coconut. Seal the bag and shake to tint.

3. Place the coated ice cream balls in waffle bowls. Sprinkle with the green coconut. Dollop with whipped topping. Sprinkle with the yellow coconut and licorice; top with maraschino cherries. Serve immediately.

FROSTY NOTES

_____
_____
_____
_____
_____
_____
_____
_____
_____
_____
_____
_____
_____
_____
_____
_____
_____
_____
_____
_____
_____
_____
_____
_____
_____
_____
_____
_____
_____
_____
_____
_____
_____
_____
_____
_____
_____
_____

GRILLED PINEAPPLE SUNDAES

I discovered a basic recipe for these luscious sundaes online, and I tweaked it a bit using some ideas from a friend. Everyone loves the grilled flavor.
—**ANITA BEACHY** BEALETON, VA

START TO FINISH: 10 MIN. • **MAKES:** 4 SERVINGS

- **4 fresh pineapple slices (about ½ inch thick)**
- **4 scoops coconut or vanilla ice cream**
- **1 cup whipped topping**
- **½ cup hot caramel ice cream topping, warmed**
- **¼ cup flaked coconut, toasted**

Cook the pineapple slices on an indoor grill for 2-3 minutes or until heated through. Transfer to individual serving plates. Top each pineapple slice with a scoop of ice cream and whipped topping. Drizzle with the caramel ice cream topping; sprinkle with coconut.

PEAR SUNDAES

My frosty pear treats are so quick and easy to prepare. They're on the table in 5 minutes flat!
—**MARY ANN SHOEMAKER** LOVELAND, CO

START TO FINISH: 5 MIN. • **MAKES:** 6 SERVINGS

- **1 can (29 ounces) pear halves, drained**
- **1 quart vanilla ice cream**
- **½ cup chocolate syrup**
- **½ cup sliced almonds, toasted**

Place pear halves, flat side up, in individual dessert dishes. Top with a scoop of vanilla ice cream. Drizzle with chocolate syrup; sprinkle with almonds.

Grilled Pineapple
Sundaes

PISTACHIO MERINGUE SUNDAES

Store-bought meringue cookies are a crispy counterpoint to scoops of pistachio gelato. I finish it all off with a drizzle of chocolate syrup and chopped nuts, but feel free to experiment with different ingredients.

—LISA SPEER PALM BEACH, FL

START TO FINISH: 5 MIN.
MAKES: 4 SERVINGS

2 **cups pistachio gelato or pistachio ice cream**
4 **miniature meringue cookies or vanilla wafers**
4 **teaspoons chocolate syrup**
¼ **cup finely chopped pistachios**

Scoop the pistachio gelato into four dessert dishes. Top each with a cookie and drizzle with chocolate syrup. Sprinkle with pistachios.

CINNAMON MOCHA SUNDAES

This two-serving recipe combines coffee, cocoa, whipped cream, cinnamon, cashews and more for a decadent treat.

—DIANE NEIBLING OVERLAND PARK, KS

START TO FINISH: 20 MIN.
MAKES: 2 SERVINGS

- ½ **cup sugar**
- 1 **tablespoon all-purpose flour**
- 1 **tablespoon baking cocoa**
- 2 **teaspoons ground cinnamon**
- ½ **teaspoon instant coffee granules**
- ½ **cup heavy whipping cream, divided**
- 1 **tablespoon butter**
- ¼ **teaspoon vanilla extract**
- 1 **tablespoon confectioners' sugar**
- ½ **cup coffee ice cream**
- ½ **cup chocolate ice cream**
- 2 **tablespoons salted cashews**

1. In a small saucepan, combine the first five ingredients; stir in ¼ cup heavy whipping cream. Bring to a boil over medium heat. Cook and stir for 2 minutes. Remove from the heat; stir in butter and vanilla. Set aside.

2. In a small bowl, beat the remaining cream until it begins to thicken. Add confectioners' sugar; beat until stiff peaks form. Spoon the ice cream into two dessert dishes. Top with sauce and whipped cream; sprinkle with cashews.

PEACH STRAWBERRY SUNDAES

Something special happens when you add a twist of lime juice to fresh peaches and strawberries. The burst of sweet-tangy fruit flavor is simply fantastic!

—KATHY CLEMENT APEZ, NC

START TO FINISH: 10 MIN.
MAKES: 6 SERVINGS

- 2½ **cups chopped peeled fresh peaches**
- 1 **cup fresh strawberries, quartered**
- 4½ **teaspoons sugar**
- 1 **tablespoon lime juice**
  Vanilla ice cream

In a large bowl, combine the peaches and strawberries. Combine the sugar and lime juice; pour over the fruit and gently toss to coat. Serve over ice cream.

FROSTY NOTES

Delicious
Chocolate
Sauce

Delicious
Chocolate
Sauce

SAUCY
TOPPINGS

DELICIOUS CHOCOLATE SAUCE

PREP: 5 MIN. • **COOK:** 10 MIN. + COOLING
MAKES: 4 CUPS

- ½ **cup butter, cubed**
- 4 **ounces unsweetened chocolate, chopped**
- 3 **cups sugar**
- ½ **teaspoon salt**
- 1 **can (12 ounces) evaporated milk**
- 1 **teaspoon vanilla extract**

1. In a small heavy saucepan, melt butter and chocolate over low heat; stir in sugar and salt. Gradually stir in milk; cook and stir until sugar is dissolved. Remove from heat; stir in vanilla.

2. Serve warm or at room temperature (sauce will thicken upon cooling). Store sauce, covered, in the refrigerator.

My sauce mixes up in a matter of minutes! One batch yields so much, I have plenty of extra to give out as gifts. Pair the chocolate sauce with gourmet cones and colorful toppings for a complete package!
—**DOROTHY ANDERSON** OTTAWA, KS

CINNAMON CREAM SYRUP

This versatile cinnamony sauce is great on ice cream, especially for the holidays, and it also makes a delightful topping for pancakes or waffles.

—**APRIL MADSEN** ELKO, NV

START TO FINISH: 20 MIN.
MAKES: 1⅔ CUPS

- 1 **cup sugar**
- ½ **cup light corn syrup**
- ¼ **cup water**
- ¾ **teaspoon ground cinnamon**
- ½ **cup evaporated milk**
  Ice cream

1. In a small saucepan, combine the sugar, corn syrup, water and cinnamon. Bring mixture to a boil over medium heat, stirring constantly; boil for 2 minutes without stirring. Remove from the heat. Let stand for 5 minutes.
2. Stir in evaporated milk. Serve warm or cold with ice cream. Refrigerate the leftovers.

BLUEBERRY SAUCE

When the weather's hot, I like to take a break with this luscious blueberry topping over a dish of vanilla ice cream. It's also delicious with a slice of angel food or pound cake.

—**DORIS DEZUR** EUGENE, OR

START TO FINISH: 20 MIN.
MAKES: ¾ CUP

- ¼ **cup sugar**
- 1 **teaspoon cornstarch**
  Dash salt
- ¼ **cup water**
- 1 **cup fresh or frozen blueberries**
- 1½ **teaspoons lemon juice**
- ½ **teaspoon grated lemon peel**
  Vanilla ice cream

In a small saucepan, combine the sugar, cornstarch and salt. Gradually whisk in water until smooth. Add the blueberries, lemon juice and peel; bring to a boil over medium heat, stirring constantly. Cook 2-3 minutes longer or until thickened, stirring occasionally (some berries will remain whole). Serve warm or chilled over ice cream.

> ### CORNSTARCH
>
> Cornstarch needs just a few minutes of boiling to thicken a sauce, gravy or dessert filling. As it continues to cook, the cornstarch will begin to lose its thickening power. Carefully follow the recipe for the best results.

ORANGE CARAMEL ICE CREAM SAUCE

We added a touch of orange extract to a creamy caramel sauce to make a rich homemade ice cream topping you won't find in stores. Try it drizzled over butter pecan, vanilla or chocolate ice cream.

—*TASTE OF HOME* TEST KITCHEN

PREP: 10 MIN.
COOK: 10 MIN. + CHILLING
MAKES: 1⅓ CUPS

- 1 **cup packed brown sugar**
- 1 **cup heavy whipping cream**
- ½ **cup sweetened condensed milk**
- ½ **teaspoon orange extract**
  Butter pecan ice cream

1. In a large saucepan, cook and stir brown sugar and cream over medium heat until sugar is dissolved. Bring to a boil; cook for 5 minutes or until mixture is reduced by half. Remove from the heat. Stir in milk and orange extract. Cover and refrigerate.
2. Just before serving, warm over low heat. Serve with ice cream.

Peppermint
Stick Sauce

PEPPERMINT STICK SAUCE

Turn ice cream into a special treat with this tasty sauce. Kids and adults alike will love its cool and sweet flavors.

—KELLY ANN GRAY BEAUFORT, SC

START TO FINISH: 25 MIN. • **MAKES:** 2¼ CUPS

> 1½ cups crushed peppermint candies
> 1 cup heavy whipping cream
> 1 jar (7 ounces) marshmallow creme

In a heavy saucepan, combine the crushed candies, whipping cream and marshmallow creme. Cook and stir over low heat until candy is completely melted and mixture is smooth. Store in the refrigerator.

RASPBERRY DESSERT SAUCE

This beautiful ruby-red sauce is an easy way to dress up ice cream, frozen yogurt or angel food cake. I like to keep an extra container of it in the freezer for a last-minute dessert.

—GUSTY CRUM DOVER, OH

PREP: 10 MIN. + CHILLING • **MAKES:** 1⅔ CUPS

> 1 package (10 ounces) frozen sweetened raspberries, thawed
> 1 tablespoon cornstarch
> 1 tablespoon cold water
> ¼ cup sugar
> ½ cup red currant jelly
> ¼ teaspoon orange extract
> Vanilla ice cream

1. In a blender, puree raspberries. Strain and discard seeds, reserving juice.
2. In a small saucepan, combine cornstarch and cold water until smooth; stir in raspberry juice and sugar. Bring to a boil over medium heat; cook and stir for 2 minutes or until thickened. Whisk in jelly and extract. Chill. Serve over ice cream.

FROSTY NOTES

BING CHERRY ICE CREAM SAUCE

START TO FINISH: 15 MIN.
MAKES: 4-6 SERVINGS

- 1 **can (16 ounces) pitted dark sweet cherries**
- 2 **tablespoons cornstarch**
- ¼ **teaspoon almond extract**
  Ice cream or frozen vanilla custard

1. Drain cherries, reserving juice. Combine cherry juice and cornstarch in a small saucepan.
2. Cook, stirring constantly, until thickened. Remove from the heat; stir in extract and cherries. Serve warm over ice cream.

> ## Pour this over your favorite ice cream for a sweet-tart treat!
> **—JANE THIBEAULT** OXFORD, MA

Bing Cherry
Ice Cream Sauce

BLACKBERRY BRANDY SAUCE

Pour this pretty sauce over your favorite ice cream or cheesecake. Shortbread's a good choice, too—it soaks up every last drop.

—CRYSTAL JO BRUNS ILIFF, CO

START TO FINISH: 25 MIN.
MAKES: 12 SERVINGS (¼ CUP EACH)

- 1 **cup sugar**
- 2 **tablespoons cornstarch**
- ¼ **cup cold water**
- 4 **cups fresh or frozen blackberries, thawed**
- 1 **tablespoon brandy or ½ teaspoon vanilla extract**
  Vanilla ice cream

In a large saucepan, mix sugar and cornstarch; stir in water. Add the blackberries; bring to a boil. Reduce heat; simmer, uncovered, 10-12 minutes or until sauce is thickened, stirring occasionally. Remove from heat; stir in brandy. Cool slightly. Serve with ice cream.

FRESH FRUIT SAUCE

I used to peel the fruits when making this sauce, but not anymore. The skins help hold the juicy summer fruit together when they are left on.

—KATIE KOZIOLEK HARTLAND, MN

PREP/TOTAL TIME: 10 MIN.
MAKES: 2¼ CUPS

- 1 **tablespoon cornstarch**
- 1 **cup orange juice**
- ⅓ **cup honey**
- 1 **cup sliced fresh peaches**
- 1 **cup sliced fresh plums**
  Vanilla ice cream

In a small saucepan, stir cornstarch and orange juice until smooth; add honey. Bring to a boil over medium heat; cook and stir for 1 minute or until thickened. Remove from the heat. Stir in peaches and plums. Serve with ice cream.

BUTTERSCOTCH MAPLE TOPPING

I came across this recipe when someone gave me a half-gallon of fresh maple syrup. The topping is great with vanilla ice cream.

—JANIS KELLY COLUMBIA CITY, IN

START TO FINISH: 20 MIN.
MAKES: 2½ CUPS

- 1 **cup packed brown sugar**
- 1 **cup maple syrup**
- ¼ **cup butter, cubed**
- 2 **teaspoons vanilla extract**
- 1 **teaspoon salt**
- ¾ **cup half-and-half cream**
  Vanilla ice cream

1. In a small saucepan, combine brown sugar and syrup. Bring to a boil over medium heat, stirring constantly. Cook and stir for 5 minutes.

2. Remove from the heat; stir in the butter, vanilla and salt. Let stand for 5 minutes.

3. Add cream; whisk for 1 minute or until well blended. Serve over ice cream. Refrigerate leftovers.

HOT FUDGE SAUCE

This fudgy sauce is scrumptious spooned over French vanilla ice cream and sprinkled with toasted pecans. Actually, I could eat the topping all by itself!

—KAREN WILLOUGHBY OVIEDO, FL

START TO FINISH: 15 MIN.
MAKES: ABOUT 1 CUP

- ½ **cup semisweet chocolate chips**
- 6 **tablespoons evaporated milk**
- 6 **tablespoons light corn syrup**
- ¼ **cup butter, cubed**
- ½ **teaspoon vanilla extract**

1. In a small heavy saucepan, combine the chocolate chips, milk and corn syrup. Cook and stir over low heat until chips are melted and mixture is smooth.
2. Stir in butter until melted. Cook and stir 5 minutes longer. Remove from the heat; stir in vanilla.

RASPBERRY SAUCE

My family has enjoyed this sweet and tart sauce, well-chilled, over ice cream for many years. For an extra treat, we top it all off with whipped cream.

—MARILYN COX SAYRE, PA

PREP: 15 MIN. + COOLING
MAKES: 3 CUPS

- ¼ **cup sugar**
- 2 **tablespoons quick-cooking tapioca**
- 2 **packages (10 ounces each) frozen sweetened raspberries, thawed, divided**
- ½ **cup water**
- 1 **cinnamon stick**
- ⅛ **teaspoon salt**
  Dash ground nutmeg
- ⅓ **cup lemon juice**
- 1 **tablespoon butter**
  Ice cream of your choice

1. In a large saucepan, combine the sugar and tapioca. Add one package of raspberries; stir to coat. Let stand for 15 minutes.

2. Stir in the water, cinnamon stick, salt and nutmeg. Bring to a boil over medium heat, stirring occasionally. Remove from the heat. Add lemon juice and butter; stir until butter is melted. Cool for 20 minutes.

3. Discard cinnamon stick. Gently stir in remaining raspberries. Cover and refrigerate until chilled. Serve with ice cream.

OUTRAGEOUS PEANUT BUTTER SAUCE

I developed this thick and creamy sauce in an attempt to re-create a peanut butter topping we had at a restaurant. Served over any kind of ice cream, it's to die for!

—**MARY LONG** AMHERST, VA

START TO FINISH: 10 MIN.
MAKES: 2 CUPS

- 1 **cup creamy peanut butter**
- ⅔ **cup confectioners' sugar**
- ½ **cup corn syrup**
- ¼ **cup water**
- 1 **teaspoon vanilla extract**
- ¼ **teaspoon salt**
- 1 **Nutrageous candy bar (3.4 ounces), finely chopped**

1. In a large bowl, combine the first six ingredients; fold in candy. Transfer to jars. Cover and store in a cool dark place for up to 4 weeks.

2. To serve, cook and stir in a small saucepan over medium-low heat until heated through. Serve with ice cream.

SUPER SPLIT

If you like the combo of peanut butter and bananas, use the Outrageous Sauce in a banana split with chocolate or vanilla ice cream, chopped peanuts, whipped cream and miniature peanut butter cups. Sweet!

GENERAL **INDEX**

• ALPHABETICAL **INDEX** •